DESIGN
your own
CROSS STITCH
to complement your home

DESIGN
your own
CROSS STITCH
to complement your home

Shirley Watts

MEREHURST

To Betty – in appreciation of all your patience and support over the past months, whilst I have been stitching and writing the text for this book

First published in 1997 by Merehurst Limited
Ferry House, 51–57 Lacy Road, Putney, London SW15 1PR

A catalogue record for this book is available from the British Library

Typeset and edited by Joanna Chisholm
Designed by Maggie Aldred
Photography by Lu Jeffery
Styling by Kate Hardy
Illustrations by King & King Design Associates
Colour separation by Bright Arts (HK) Limited
Printed in Italy by Olivotto

CONTENTS

INTRODUCTION

Cross stitch is an old and noble form of embroidery, employed from time immemorial to decorate household linen and clothing. The origins of cross stitch are lost in the mists of time, but we do know that very early sewing stitches resembling cross stitch were used by primitive man, who worked upon skins rather than fabric. Since these early times, cross stitch has become more sophisticated, and it has firmly established a place for itself in the world of embroidery, every generation adding something fresh to the skill.

Being firmly of the opinion that you can create the best designs from things that appeal to you personally, some of my examples in this book are inevitably influenced by images from nature. I hope, however, that I have also demonstrated many ways in which ideas, patterns and colour, gleaned from our homes and further afield, can provide equally strong inspiration for designs, and how my simple techniques can be used to create embroideries to appeal to a wide variety of tastes.

This book is written for the cross stitcher with some basic experience. The early chapters, however, begin with very simple ideas, and my aim has been to stretch these existing basic skills to create something beautiful, and with a special personal appeal.

Cross stitchers tend to be creatures of habit. The most common project is one worked on a piece of 14-count or 18-count Aida fabric and is embroidered in stranded cotton, yet over the last few years, in particular, a wealth of new fabrics has become available in a variety of counts and in a riot of colours. As well as using fabrics, we can work our cross stitch on other materials – silk gauze, paper, canvas, plastic canvas and vinyl weave. Nor is the cross stitcher any longer tied to stranded cottons. There are metallic threads, flower threads, silk threads, rayon threads, variagated threads, various types of wools and even ribbons. The amazing variety of materials available presents an exciting challenge.

Ideas and inspiration can be found in the wealth of designs that have come down to us through the ages from the Mediterranean, northern Europe, North America and Asia. Having looked at some of these, let us take a walk around our own home and seek out a few of our favourite things – a treasured piece of china, a pretty wallpaper, an attractive furnishing fabric, a stencil decoration, stylish tiles – which can provide the visual images to inspire us to create beautiful coordinating accessories. Whether the designs are simple or complex, let us see what, with a little bit of skill, a lot of enthusiasm and a large helping of imagination, we can create for ourselves.

PLAYING WITH SIMPLE PATTERNS

Whenever I suggest to a group of embroiderers that it would be great fun to design their own cross stitch patterns, I inevitably get the same response: 'It's all right for you ... you can draw'. Whilst I would not deny that drawing skills are useful when creating some kinds of design, there are many styles that require no drawing ability whatsoever. To illustrate this, neither of the designs in this chapter needs any artistic skills, and even if you have never tried making your own patterns before, you can create your very own designs and select colours to match or complement your own particular décor.

I have begun with some very simple geometric flower motifs, including stalks and a few geometric leaves, and then added a border. This kind of design would be suitable for any square or rectangular area, large or small. You might, for example, want to tackle something as large as a cushion for a chair or a telephone seat, or as small as a notebook cover or a small bookmark. I chose two medium-sized projects – a visitors' book cover and a bellpull – which I thought might go together in a front porch or hallway. In each of these designs there are only four shades of the same colour, plus green for the leaves.

If you wish to work my designs first, before attempting your own, you can simply alter the colours to suit your own colour preferences. To make the bellpull and the visitors' book match, just substitute the four shades of blue for the four shades of red – navy for maroon, light navy for light maroon, blue for red and light blue for pink in the key – or vise versa. Alternatively, if you would rather change the colours completely to complement the décor of your own porch or hallway, this is always possible too.

Manufacturer's Shade Cards

Just as when choosing paint you consult a colour card, so when selecting embroidery thread it is possible to look at a manufacturer's shade card. These cards, which carry samples of each colour available in a particular type of thread, are invaluable to the designer. All the shades of a particular colour are shown as a run – from the lightest to the darkest. It is possible to select the required number of colours that will blend with each other and provide a progression of colour. You may want to do your embroidery in red, but not the particular shades of red that I have chosen. On the colour card you will find runs of orangy reds, browny reds, purply reds and so on. The same is true for autumn colours such as yellows, oranges and golden browns, for rich purples, lilacs and mauves, for leafy shades of green, bluish greens, yellowy greens, dull greens and bright greens. The choice is yours. With the appropriate shade cards it is possible to find the

nearest equivalent of a colour in six-stranded embroidery cotton, or other types of thread.

All good needlework shops should have copies of these colour cards, but if you wish to purchase one of your own, it would be best to contact the main distributor of the threads you want to use. You will find some useful addresses and telephone numbers of suppliers at the end of this book.

Types of Thread

Two types of embroidery cotton are used in this chapter: six- and single-stranded cotton. Six-stranded embroidery cotton is the very versatile thread with which you will be most familiar. As its name suggests it can be split into six separate strands, and can be used in one, two or three strands on most evenweave materials. On coarser fabrics, however, you may need more strands to cover the material adequately. This type of thread has a soft sheen and is very easy to use.

Single-stranded embroidery cotton – sometimes known as 'flower thread' – is a matte, pure cotton thread, twisted into a single soft strand. The original flower threads came from Denmark, but other major manufacturers now make a similar sort of embroidery cotton. It was called flower thread because the colour range of the original Danish threads was based largely on the exquisite flower designs of the Danish designer Gerda Bengtsson and from the colours in traditional Danish embroidery. The range of colours on the market now is much wider and mirrors, to a large extent, the colours available in six-stranded cotton.

Marrying Thread With Material

Aida is an evenweave material that has a blocked structure. The weft and the warp threads are bunched to form squares of solid material, with distinct needle holes at the corners of each block, which makes counting of squares easy. Aida is available in various 'counts'. The count is the number of holes per 2.5cm (1in). In some cross stitch patterns you will come across the abbreviation hpi, which stands for 'holes per inch' – the equivalent of 'count'.

For the visitors' book project, I have used the popular 18-count cream Aida, which is a fairly fine evenweave. I have used single-stranded cotton for this project, but if you wanted to embroider with six-stranded thread I would recommend two strands. Three strands would barely go through the holes and would result in a bulky ugly effect; whereas one strand would give a very light open finish.

Jobelan is also an evenweave material, but in contrast to Aida the threads are evenly spaced. Counting the threads has to be done with great care, and I would recommend using a magnifying glass. Made from a mixture of 51 per cent cotton and 49 per cent modal, Jobelan is a lovely soft material, suitable not only for embroidered pictures and bellpulls but also for many household projects such as tablecloths, place mats, napkins and cushion covers. It is available in about 50 beautiful and subtle shades. For the bellpull I have used 28-count Jobelan. Because Jobelan is usually stitched over two threads, the 28-count material is the equivalent of a 14 count to work on, and although the stitches are the same size as those on 14-count Aida, the background is a fine-textured one.

On the bellpull I have used three strands of six-stranded embroidery cotton because flower thread was too fine for my purpose and the three strands of stranded cotton gave a more appropriate, firm, solid effect. For finer work on table linen I sometimes use only two strands on Jobelan, as you will find in later projects in this book. Two strands is better in some instances when you want to preserve the soft supple character of the fabric.

There are no hard and fast rules as to how

many strands of thread to use. The three worked samples on this and the next page demonstrate different finishes, resulting from the use of stranded embroidery cotton and single-strand embroidery cotton, on three different types of material.

On the 14-count Aida sample, the top row is worked in three strands of six-stranded embroidery cotton for a solid finish, which completely covers the fabric. Each cross merges into the next, bringing out the full colour of the thread. When steam pressed on the back, the embroidery is raised above the surface of the material on the right side, giving an almost three-dimensional appearance.

The middle row is stitched with two strands of six-stranded embroidery cotton. This gives a lighter, more open finish, where the form of each individual cross stitch is clear. The fabric shows through when dark thread is worked on light-coloured Aida. If stitching with a light thread on dark-coloured Aida, the dark material will also be

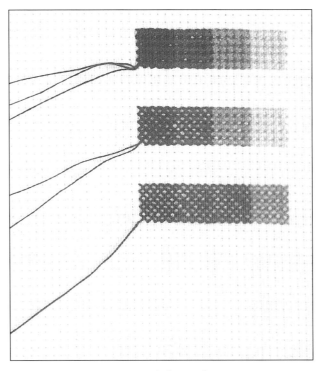

14-count Aida sample

evident. Using only two strands on 14-count Aida dilutes the colour of the thread, too. Bear this in mind when you are designing, and choosing colours.

The bottom row of the 14-count Aida sample is worked with single-stranded embroidery cotton (flower thread or Nordin), which is about the same thickness as two threads of stranded cotton, and so the finish is similar. It is, however, easier to get a smoother flatter appearance to your cross stitch as there is only the one strand. This avoids the problem of strands twisting around one another.

On the 18-count Aida sample, the top row is stitched with two strands of six-stranded embroidery cotton. This gives a solid finish on this finer material and completely covers the fabric. Two threads also bring out the full colour of the cotton on this fabric.

In the middle row I have used one strand of six-stranded embroidery cotton for a lighter, more open look. The form of each cross stitch is

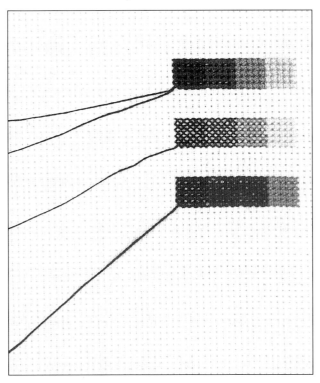

18-count Aida sample

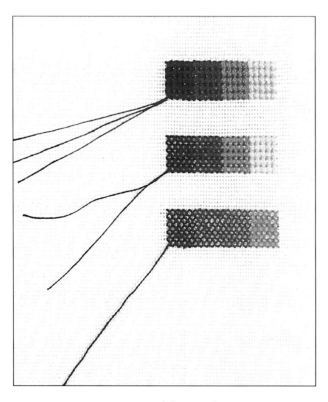

28-count Jobelan sample

The middle row shows two strands of six-stranded embroidery cotton worked over two threads of the Jobelan. Such a light finish is often very appropriate on this fine soft material. The only disadvantage is that the colours may appear slightly muted, and you may wish to compensate for this when you choose colours for your design.

The single-stranded embroidery cotton, used in the bottom row of the 28-count Jobelan sample, is similar in thickness to two strands of the six-stranded cotton. It produces a light even finish, and is ideal for delicate designing.

My samples show only some of the effects that can be achieved. I suggest, however, that before creating and working your own designs you work a few practice pieces, using assorted threads and different numbers of thread on various materials. This will help you to achieve the look you have in mind.

clear, but when working with dark shades on light material, or with light thread on dark material, the colour of the Aida shows through. Another thing to note is that the depth of thread colour is diluted, when compared with the effect gained by using two strands on the same material.

The bottom row of the 18-count Aida sample is stitched with single-stranded embroidery cotton. A single strand covers this material much better than the 14-count fabric, and the finer stitch brings out the full colour of the thread.

The 28-count Jobelan sample has the top row stitched with three strands of six-stranded embroidery cotton, worked over two threads of the material. Such a finish is similar to that on the 14-count Aida fabric, although the background material is finer and less rigid than the Aida. For a firm heavy look, such as is required for the bellpull, three strands are ideal, but for a lighter finish – for the table linen, for example – two strands would be more supple.

VISITORS' BOOK COVER

The visitors' book cover measures
21.5cm x 16.5cm (8¹/₂in x 6¹/₂in)

YOU WILL NEED
18-count cream Aida fabric, 71cm x 25cm (28in x 10in)
White or cream lining fabric, 71cm x 25cm (28in x 10in)
Single-stranded embroidery cotton as given in the key
No 26 tapestry needle
Visitors' book measuring 20cm x 15cm (8in x 6in)

This project has been stitched in
DMC flower threads

The Embroidery

1 Fold the Aida in half, giving a working area of 35.5cm x 25cm (14in x 10in). With the fold on the left, measure in 19mm (3/4in) and baste from top to bottom. From this line, count 137 squares to your right and baste another line from top to bottom. This will be the width of the design.

2 Find the centre point of the rectangle formed

by the two lines of basting stitches and the top and bottom edge of the material. This central point is the best place at which to begin your embroidery.

3 Find the centre point of the chart, thread your needle with one strand of your single-stranded thread and begin stitching.

4 Steam press on the wrong side when complete.

Finishing the Visitors' Book

1 With the right side of the embroidery face down, turn in a narrow hem all round the edge and press. Ensure that the book jacket just covers the top and bottom edges of the visitors' book.

2 Centre the lining fabric on the back of the Aida and fold in a narrow hem, covering all the raw edges of the Aida. Baste into position so that the lining fabric comes to within 6mm (1/4in) of the folded edge of the Aida. Stitch the lining into position.

3 Centre the book on the wrong side of the fabric and fold the extra width over the front and back side edges of the cover. Topstitch through the folds at the top and bottom to form pockets.

VISITORS' BOOK COVER

		DMC FLOWER THREADS	ANCHOR NORDIN
T	Maroon	2902	897
l	Red	2304	47
+	Pink	2899	40
·	Light maroon	2815	65
⊼	Bluish-green	2502	209

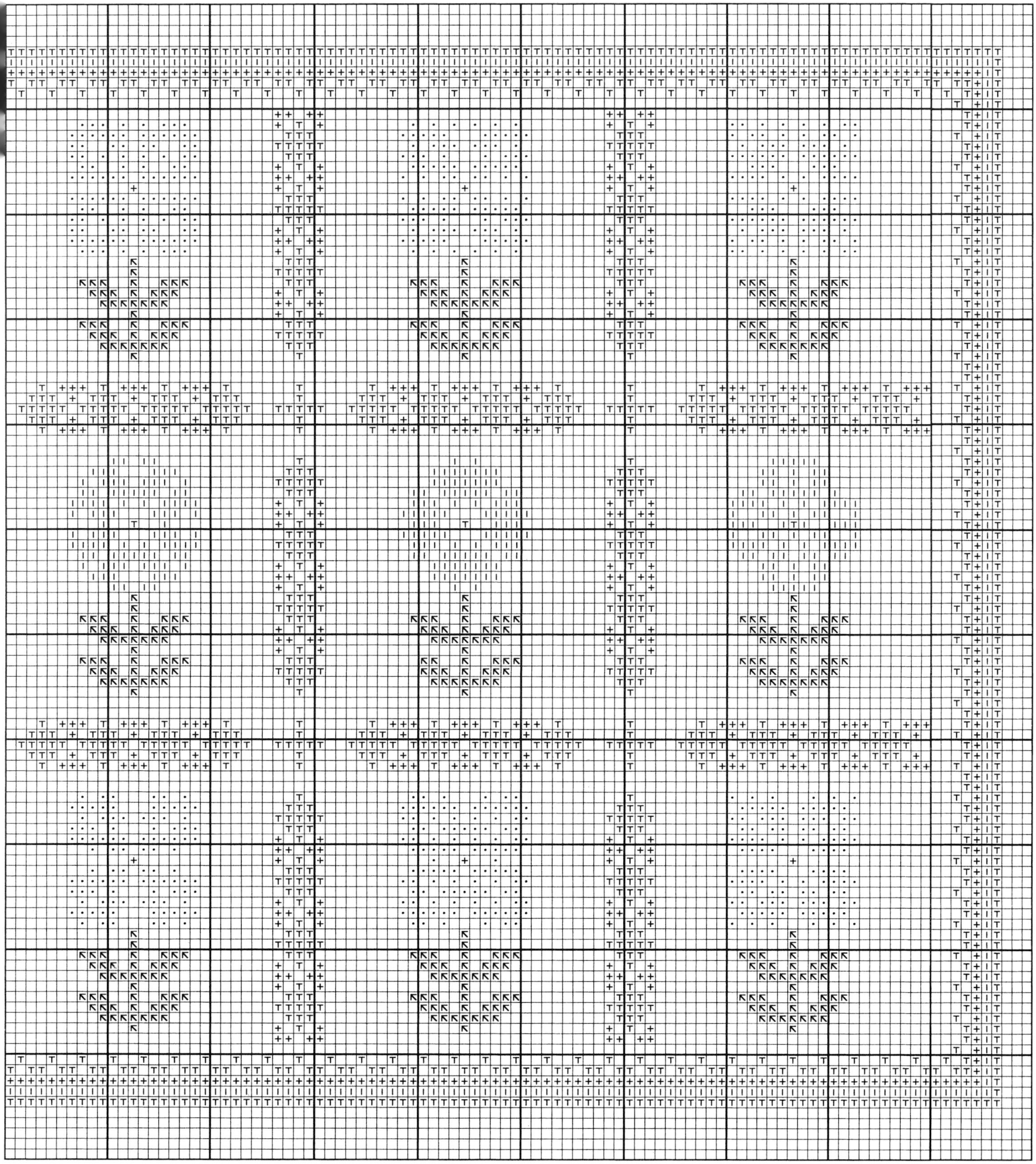

BELLPULL

**The finished bellpull measures
38cm x 10cm (15in x 4in)**

YOU WILL NEED

*28-count ivory Jobelan fabric, 48cm x 20cm (19in x 8in)
Cream lining fabric, 48cm x 20cm (19in x 8in)
Iron-on interfacing, 38cm x 10cm (15in x 4in)
Stranded embroidery cotton as given in the key
No 24 tapestry needle
Pair of bellpull rods, 10cm (4in) wide
Bell (optional)*

This project has been stitched in
DMC six-stranded embroidery cotton

The Embroidery

1 Find the centre of your piece of Jobelan, and find the centre of your bellpull pattern.

2 Begin stitching at this point, using three strands of thread in the needle.

3 Gently steam press on the wrong side when complete.

Finishing the Bellpull

1 Centre the interfacing on the back of the embroidery and iron into position.

2 Trim the long edges until the piece measures 13cm (5in) across. Make sure that the borders along each side of the embroidery are of equal width. Turn in the long edges by 12mm (1/2in) and press. Trim the cream lining fabric to the same width, and turn in along the long edge.

3 Baste the lining fabric so that it covers the raw edge of the Jobelan and comes to within 6mm (1/4in) of the outside long edge of the bellpull. Repeat on the other long edge, and then neatly slipstitch into position.

4 Trim the short edges until the piece measures 43cm (17in) long. This time, make sure that the borders along the top and bottom of the

embroidery are of equal depth. On the two short edges, make a 6mm (1/4in) turning.

5 Make a second turning 2cm (3/4in), taking the fabric over a rod at the top and bottom. Baste, and then neatly slipstitch in place.

6 Make a tassel 10cm (4in) long from any combination of colours in your embroidery, using the six-stranded thread. Cut lengths of thread 20cm (8in) long, thread them through the ring on the lower rod of the bellpull and bind them around the top with another length of six-stranded cotton, and neatly stitch in the ends.

BELLPULL

		DMC	ANCHOR	MADEIRA
+	Light navy	336	149	1006
Z	Navy	939	127	1009
U	Blue	322	978	1004
/	Pale blue	827	160	1014
−	Green	3815	877	1704

The chart for the bellpull
has been split over two
pages. The upper part
(Section A) is on this
page, while the lower part
(Section B) appears on the
page opposite

Section A

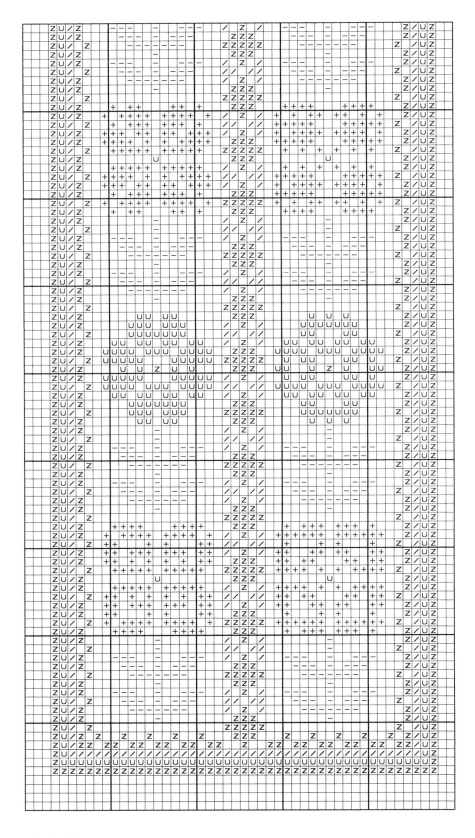

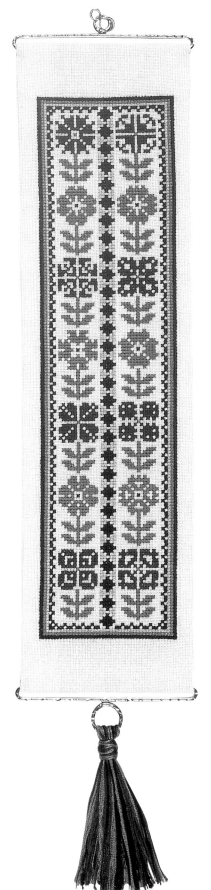

Section B

DESIGNING YOUR OWN FLOWERS

T he idea for creating geometric flower motifs came to me when I was looking at some very attractive Palestinian embroideries incorporating the rose or rosette motif. These simple geometric motifs are designed within a block of squares. Each square represents a stitch. For the flower head I decided on a 13 by 13 square block because this was the size that best fitted the final size of my design. In theory it would be possible to create a motif within any block, as long as the number of squares along the top and sides was an odd number.

If you examine the visitors' book cover and bellpull, you will notice that there are two basic designs: Flower A, in which the 'flowers' worked in darker thread have four petals with their tips pointing towards the corners of the block; Flower B, in which the 'flowers' worked in lighter thread have four petals, but the centre point of these is in the centre of each of the four sides of the block.

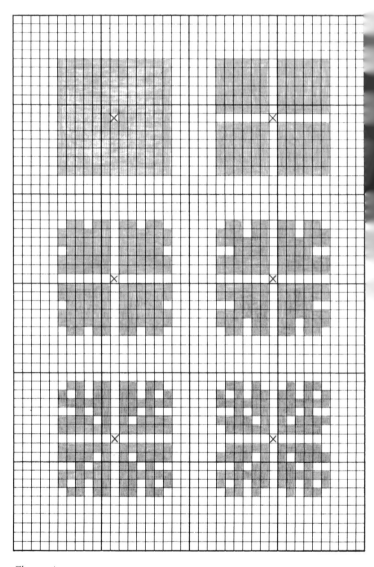

Flower A

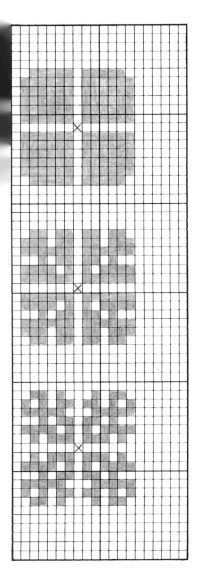

Flower B

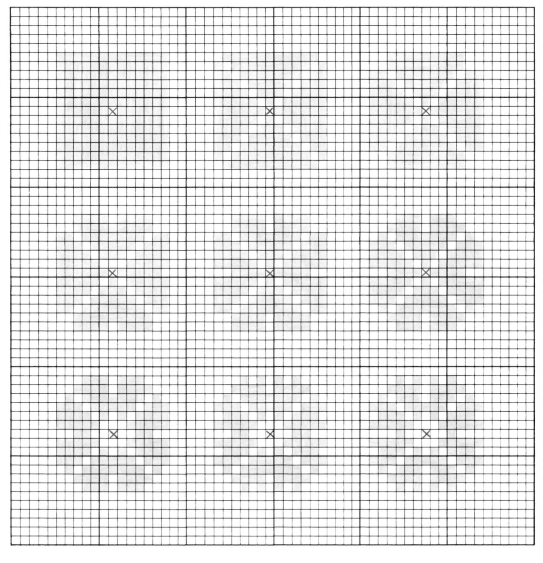

Graph paper, 10 squares to the 2.5cm (1in), large enough to accommodate the number of motifs you wish to design (One complete flower motif fills 23 squares down by 13 squares across)
Sharp HB pencil
Soft eraser
Coloured crayons

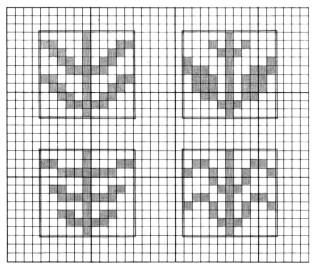

Flower stalk and leaves

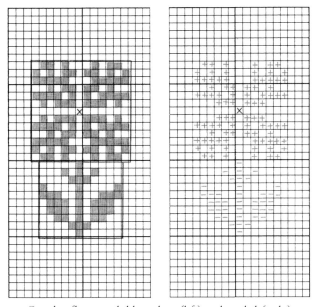

Complete flower, coded by colour (left) and symbol (right)

Flower Head A

1 On your piece of graph paper, use a coloured crayon to make a mark in every square within a 13 by 13 square block except the centre square.

2 Mark the centre square with a cross.

3 From the centre, carefully erase the six squares above, below, to the left and to the right of this centre square. This leaves the four 'petals' of your flower.

4 Remove one or two squares at a time, systematically from each of the four petals. Ensure that all the petals are symmetrical. You can remove as many or as few squares as you like, as long as you preserve your flower shape. I am not a mathematician, so I cannot tell you how many different combinations of squares are possible. Can you spot any two alike on my two designs?

Flower Head B

Follow the same procedure as for Flower head A except for step 3. Instead of removing the six squares above, below and to either side of the centre, remove the six squares to each corner.

Flower Stalk and Leaves

1 On your piece of graph paper, outline a block 10 squares down by 11 squares across.

2 Mark in the stalk – the ten squares down through the centre of the block, using the pencil.

3 Keeping your shapes symmetrical on either side of the central stalk, block in your leaf shapes, using the figure top left to give you some ideas.

4 When you are satisfied with your design, join it up with one of your flower heads, so that the top of the flower stalk touches the bottom of the flower head motif at the centre.

5 Redraw your complete motif on clean graph paper. This time you can use crayons to colour in squares representing stitches of different colours, or you can use symbols. For each design you will

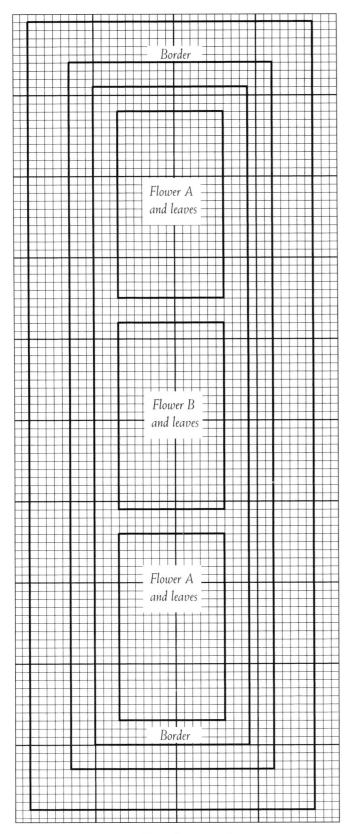

Using flower motifs

need three colours: for petals, flower centre and leaves. Complete with a key.

USING FLOWER MOTIFS

Having created your own flower motifs, it is relatively easy to transfer the designs on to the project of your choice – for example, to create your own bookmark design or an insert for a larger item.

YOU WILL NEED
Material of your choice, at least 10cm x 25cm (4in x 10in)
Iron-on interfacing, at least 10cm x 25cm (4in x 10in)
Embroidery cotton of your choice
Graph paper, 10 squares to the 2.5cm (1in),
at least 40 x 100 squares in total
Sharp HB pencil
Soft eraser
Coloured crayons

Design Techniques

1 On a piece of graph paper, mark off 97 squares down by 35 squares across.

2 Design two of Flower A and one of Flower B.

3 Arrange the flowers one above the other on the graph paper, leaving 11 squares at the top and bottom, three squares between the motifs and 11 squares on the left- and right-hand sides.

4 Leaving an outer margin of five squares all-round, design an inner border that will be three squares wide. Creating such a border is a job that can be done satisfactorily only by trial and error, and your pencil and your eraser will be your most useful tools here. Line borders and very simple borders present few problems, but more complex ones with complicated repeat patterns often raise difficulties at the corners. On the next page I have included a few ideas – simple borders, progressing to more complex ones, which may trigger off ideas of your own.

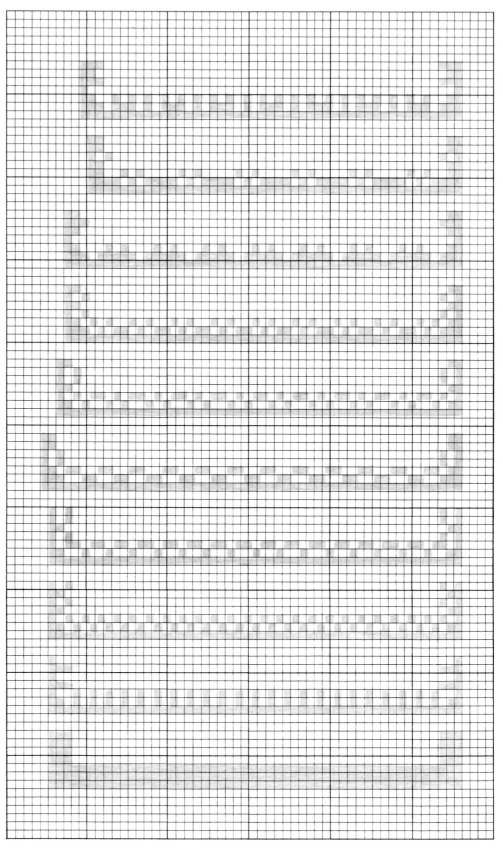

Border patterns

5 Decide on whether you are going to work on 18-count Aida or on 28-count Jobelan, and then calculate the size of the finished project as follows.

> Number of stitches ÷ Count of material = Size, in inches, which are then converted into centimetres.

If the pattern is 97 squares (stitches) long and 35 squares (stitches) wide, the following calculations should be made on 18-count Aida:

> Length 97 ÷ 18 = 5.4in = 13.5cm

In the same way, work out the width of the project:

> Width 35 ÷ 18 = 1.9in = 5cm

On 28-count Jobelan (remember that you are working over two threads, so the effective count is 14):

> Length 97 ÷ 14 = 6.9in = 17.5cm

> Width 35 ÷ 14 = 2.5in = 6.5cm

6 Cut out your piece of material, allowing 3.5cm (1½in) extra all the way round.

7 Stitch your design. If you are unsure of how to do this, refer back to the visitors' book and the bellpull earlier in the chapter to check on the type of thread and the number of strands to use with your material.

8 When complete, steam press on the wrong side and back with iron-on interfacing. You may want to machine around the finished edge of the project and fringe the edges.

RICH DESIGNS FROM KILIMS

In pursuit of inspiration for our next projects, we shall be taking off on our magic carpet towards the eastern Mediterranean and central Asia – the homeland of the kilim. 'Kilim' is the Turkish for a flatweave rug – that is a rug without a knotted pile. Kilims are traditionally made by tribes of nomadic herders, on very simple, horizontal ground looms that can easily be dismantled and transported. They are made from homespun wool, collected from the nomads' own sheep, with, sometimes, the hair from goats and camels added for extra strength and lustre. Kilims are fast becoming one of the most fashionable and striking features of Western interior design and their spectacular colours immediately catch the eye.

Traditionally, natural dyes are used. These are obtained from flower petals, fruit skins, vegetables, roots, bark, leaves, insects such as the cochineal, and even earth. Modern, chemically dyed threads are unable to capture the softness and subtlety of colour that these central Asian herders achieve, yet they still produce some rich terracottas, indigos, yellows, oranges, browns and creams, so we can do our best.

The patterns woven into these flatweave carpets are predominantly abstract ones – geometric patterns incorporating stepped shapes, crenellations, diamond medallions and triangles, together with stylised shapes of trees, flower petals and leaves. Some of the motifs commonly used in kilims must pre-date Islamic influence in the area. Because the belief that only God can create a living thing was strictly enforced by the Islamic faith, any realism in representation was vigorously suppressed. You will notice that there is no light and shade in kilim designs, no perspective, no attempt to create a picture, no reality. Some pre-Islamic images, however, have been allowed to remain – camels, goats, sheep and even human figures – but they always appear in isolation as part of a pattern, never as part of a pictorial scene.

In my designs for the desk tidy and pot cover I have tried to capture some of the spirit of these very distinctive patterns. The desk tidy comprises two kilims for the pens and pencils and a simple geometric border of triangles for the paper clip tray. On the larger of the two kilims, a bold geometric pattern forms the borders and through the centre panel runs a line of scorpion or spider motifs. On the smaller kilim, a fine zig-zag pattern forms the borders, and the centre panel contains diamond-shaped medallions, all with the same pattern but embroidered in different colours. On the band for the pot cover, a geometric pattern of terracotta, yellow and brown diamonds and triangles

alternates with a primitive representation of a goat.

In these few simple designs it would be impossible to include all the traditional symbols and patterns that form the rich 'tapestry' of kilims. This means, however, that there is plenty of scope for you to design your own!

Vinyl Weave

Vinyl weave is a very strong but pliable, 14-count, white vinyl evenweave material. It can be wrapped around cylindrical or oval tubs, boxes or tubes, and will not spring open – as more rigid plastic canvas does. Because vinyl weave is double threaded, you can do three-quarter stitches on it. However, it does not 'give' as a fabric does, so may resist a threaded needle. Vinyl weave could be used for place settings or coasters as it can be washed and wiped and is virtually indestructible. It also cuts easily with scissors to any shape, but it will not tear.

DESK TIDY
PAPER CLIP TRAY

		MADEIRA	DMC	ANCHOR
Y	Red	0407	347	13
K	Green	1205	561	212

DESK TIDY

**The finished desk tidy measures
10cm (4in) high and 18cm (7in) across**

YOU WILL NEED
*1 sheet of 14-count vinyl weave fabric
Stranded embroidery cotton as given in the key
No 24 tapestry needle
Matching sewing cotton
Stout card in a colour of your choice, for the base
Cardboard tube, 5cm (2in) diameter, with a plastic lid at
each end, available from stationery shops
Craft knife
Tube of glue
Rubber bands*

This project has been stitched in
Madeira six-stranded embroidery cotton

The Embroidery

1 Begin your embroidery in the first available hole from the bottom edge of your vinyl weave. Even though this material is very strong and you can be very economical with it, it is still advisable to leave a few extra holes at either end of your 'carpet strip' in case your cardboard tube is slightly bigger than the one I used. In this case you may have to add a few vertical rows to the design to cover the tube. I worked with two strands of embroidery cotton in the needle. With the darker colours this seemed to give a rather light covering of the vinyl, but three strands would have been too bulky.

2 When the embroidery is finished, cut along the

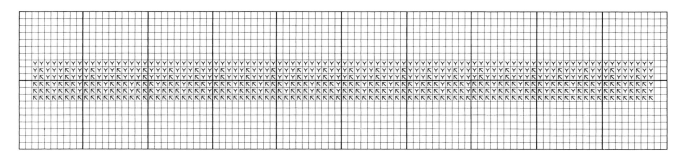

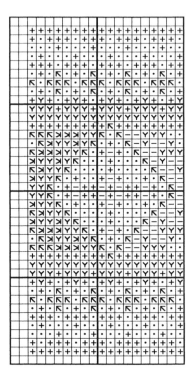

DESK TIDY:
MEDIUM KILIM

		MADEIRA	DMC	ANCHOR
⊞	Light navy	1006	311	149
⊵	Blue	1106	518	168
Y	Red	0407	347	13
◥	Green	1205	561	212
·	Cream	0111	3078	292
–	Yellow	0106	444	291

DESK TIDY:
LARGE KILIM

		MADEIRA	DMC	ANCHOR
⊓	Light navy	1006	311	149
⊵	Blue	1106	518	168
Y	Red	0407	347	13
◥	Green	1205	561	212
·	Cream	0111	3078	292
–	Yellow	0106	444	291

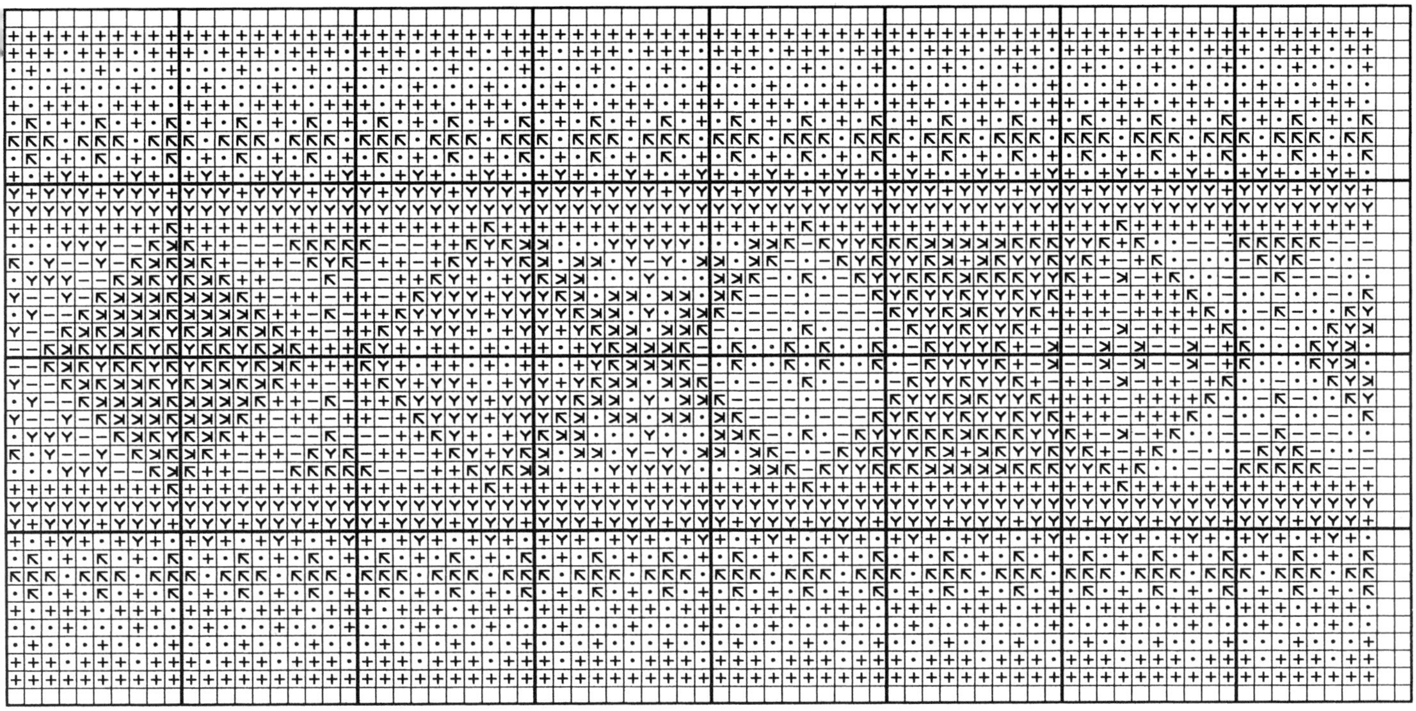

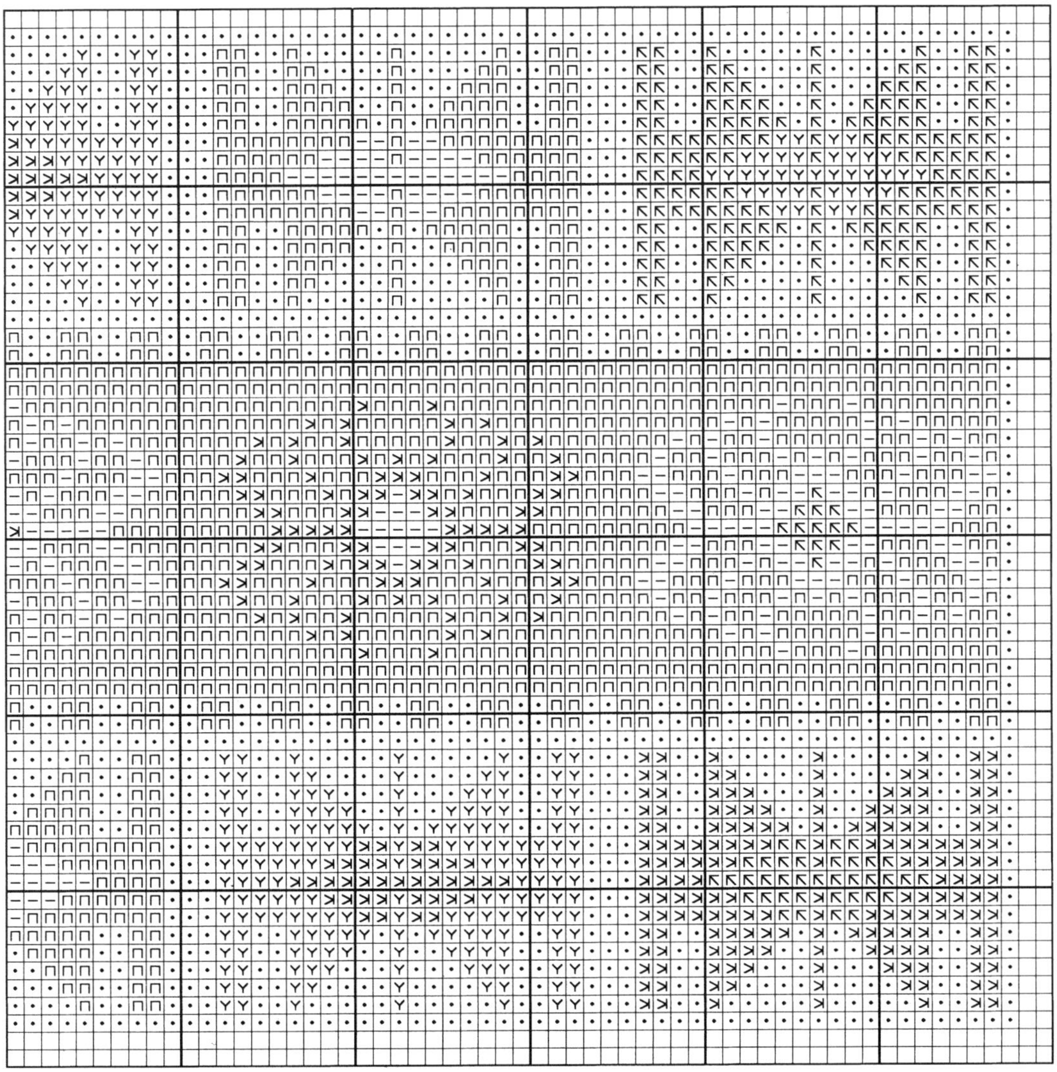

long edge on the first line of holes beyond your stitching. Do not cut down the short edges until you have placed your vinyl around your cardboard tube and ascertained that it is wide enough to meet at the back!

3 Complete all three pieces in the same way.

Finishing the Desk Tidy

1 Along the short, left-hand side of each of the two bigger pieces, using two strands of matching or complementary coloured embroidery cotton, make a knotted fringe. Clip to about 2.5cm (1in) long when complete.

2 Remove the plastic lid at each end of the cardboard tube. Using a sharp craft knife, cut three pieces of cardboard tubing 6mm ($1/4$in) shorter than the piece of embroidered vinyl. If you now insert one of the plastic lids in the bottom of each of the two bigger tubes, it will make them easier to stick down to the base later, and it will lift your tube so that it is now only marginally shorter than the embroidery. I found a third plastic lid to put in the paper clip tray, but this depends on what you have available. It is not essential.

3 Stick each piece of embroidery around its matching piece of tubing, using rubber bands to hold it until set hard. I carefully stitched behind the fringes as well, to make sure of a secure finish.

4 With a craft knife, cut your base to shape – if you want one – and then glue your tubes in place.

POT COVER

The finished pot cover measures
20cm (8in) high and 61.5cm (24$1/2$in) around
the circumference

YOU WILL NEED
28-count sage-green Jobelan fabric,
50cm x 76cm (18in x 30in)
Sage-green lining fabric, 50cm x 76cm (18in x 30in)
Stranded embroidery cotton as given in the key
Matching sewing cotton
No 24 tapestry needle
1m (1yd) matching green fringe, 2.5cm (1in) deep
Straight-sided, metal container, 20cm (8in) high

This project has been stitched in
Madeira six-stranded embroidery cotton

The Embroidery

1 Before you begin your embroidery, measure the height of your pot, and mark out on your Jobelan fabric, using basting stitches, the position of the top and bottom edges of your pot.

2 Then measure the circumference of the pot, and demarcate with basing stitches the width of material required to go around the pot.

3 Cut away any surplus, leaving at least 5cm (2in) beyond your basting line along the bottom and down each side of your material, and at least 7.5cm (3in) extra across the top.

4 Mark the centre point along the top row of basting stitches, and measure down 2.5cm (1in). Mark the spot with basting stitches.

5 Find the centre of the top row of your pattern; this is the best place to begin. Use two strands of embroidery cotton in the needle.

6 Continue the repeat pattern across your material until you have a strip that will go completely around your pot and meet at the back.

7 Steam press on the back when complete.

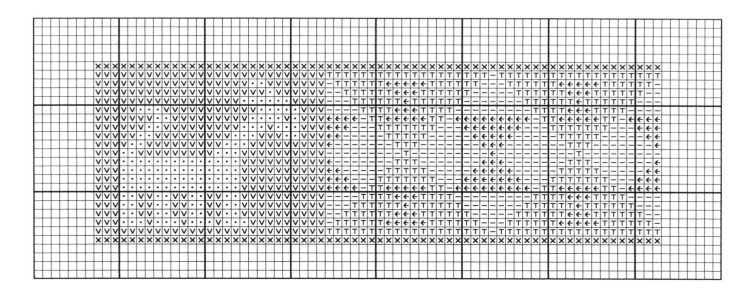

Finishing the Pot Cover

1 With the right side of the embroidery and the right side of the lining fabric together, machine stitch along the top edge 3.5cm (1¹/₂in) above the basting line marking the top edge of the pot. Turn the embroidery to the right side and press flat along the stitched line.

2 Fold the material in half, lining side in, and after checking it around the pot, machine up the seam at the back.

3 Turn up the hem along the bottom line of basting stitches. Trim the lining and turn in the raw edge to cover the raw edge of the Jobelan. Hem neatly.

4 Slide the cover over the pot, so that it just covers the lower edge of the pot at the bottom. Fold over the excess material at the top, and mark the line of the top of the pot. It should be marked

POT COVER			
	MADEIRA	DMC	ANCHOR
☒ Orange	0114	742	303
⊟ Yellow	0104	307	289
⊤ Brick-red	0314	918	341
☑ Dark green	1514	520	862
⊡ Cream	0111	3078	292
⮘ Dark brown	2004	3371	382

by your original line of basting stitches, but it is worth checking!

5 A typical kilim includes a fringe. To include a fringe around your pot cover, pin your fringe in place and stitch neatly in position. It should just clear the top of your embroidered band.

Adapting these designs

*T*he pot cover band could be altered to decorate a shopping bag, belt or even the bottom of a skirt. Any of the three strips from either of the pens and pencils kilims could, with a little bit of adjustment, be worked end on to produce a similar band. Just use a piece of graph paper to rearrange the motifs to suit yourself.

Creating your own kilim borders

If you are fortunate enough to own a kilim or have brought back textiles with similar motifs from far-away places, you can easily translate the patterns into a cross stitch design. It is a good idea to start with geometric shapes to make simple borders, and these can be used to embellish many items around the home. Modern kilim weavers use not only traditional motifs but also ones based on contemporary household items such as kettles, teapots, combs and lamps. They also incorporate objects showing Western influence such as cars and bikes, helicopters and even, sadly, rifles. Kilim motifs are always represented as very simplified, two-dimensional shapes, so they do not need great drawing skills.

YOU WILL NEED
Graph paper, 10 squares to the 2.5cm (1in), large enough to accommodate the number of motifs you wish to design
Sharp HB pencil
Soft eraser
Coloured crayons

---

1 Pick out a simple motif or geometric shape from your kilim and draw it on to the graph paper.
2 Many motifs will follow the grid of the graph paper, but if necessary modify the outline by redrawing over it along the squares, as this represents where your cross stitches will go.
3 Repeat your design on a horizontal line across the graph paper, allowing the same amount of space between single motifs.
4 Colour in your design with one of the shades you have picked out from the kilim, and then the complementary band of colour behind the design for a simple border.
5 You can develop your design by placing several bands together or by alternating one motif with another in the same band. Try bands of different widths for the best effects.

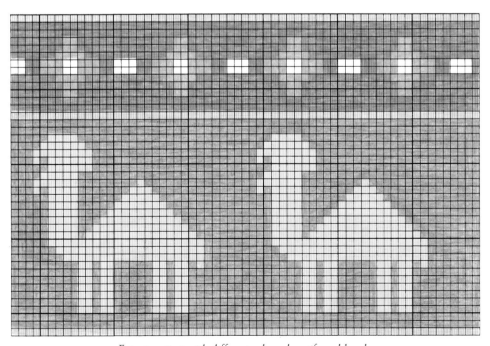
Experimenting with different coloured motifs and bands

FOLK ART MOTIFS

When settlers first made their homes in America, they had to create a comfortable lifestyle for themselves with only a limited supply of materials. Chairs and beds were therefore enhanced with beautifully stitched quilts in an infinite variety of patterns and colours. Pretty curtains were transformed from cheap plain cotton or calico gingham, while settees became more inviting through the addition of cushions, sometimes square, sometimes heart shaped, often in bright check materials. Samplers, large wall hangings or stencilled designs of flowers and foliage covered bare walls. Furniture, chests and boxes were also stencilled or hand painted with stylised flowers and fruits, leaves and hearts.

Similar folk art fun motifs are to be found in rural Scandinavia, where cheerful stylised designs of roses, daisies, lilies and tulips are painted freehand on furniture, cradles and kitchenware. Stencilled patterns enhance door panels, door frames and the walls of homes, while comfortable woven or tapestry cushions and rugs, as well as colourful wall hangings and table coverings in traditional patterns, all give the home a warm and inviting feel.

Amidst the cold, clinical, abstract world of high technology in which we find ourselves today, there is a move in some quarters to recreate this simple, welcoming and homely country style of decoration in living rooms, where family and friends can gather in comfort. I have therefore chosen a few of the recurring motifs from this style of decoration and created a group of five simple designs that, when worked, would not look out of place in a country home.

For the sampler design I just let my imagination run riot. I incorporated four of the most common elements in folk art – the star, the checks, the heart and the bow – and then added three little elves for a bit of fun. Perhaps the most popular single image in quilting is the star, of which inevitably there are hundreds of designs, although stars generally have five, six or eight points. In my sampler, the three calico stars, based on the Lemoyne Star, are composed of fabric-like diamonds. This type of star was named after the two brothers Jean Baptiste and Pierre Lemoyne, who founded New Orleans in 1718. Another favourite pattern is gingham, which in the sampler is to be found in the green blocks and blue stars. Against the green check is the ever-present heart motif of folk design. Hearts are common in all colours of check, plain and patterned material, and I felt that the heart must feature on my sampler. Bows are also popular and so I included some red bows above the rods where Scandinavian-style

'little people' ride as on a carousel, each suspended from a star.

For the key box I chose the 'spinning star' motif, suggested by a delightful American quilt, sewn in Texas about 1840. The quilt was made of fabric scraps, each piece a different colour. I have tried to recreate this rare pattern, which is so full of movement, in cross stitch – not an easy task because of all the different angles involved, but I hope it will inspire you to try your hand at creating a cross stitch design, to complement your own quilt perhaps!

The key fob designs are much simpler. Two of them are based on the check patterns that are so much a part of country design, and of course the colours can be changed to suit your taste. The third luggage tag or key fob is decorated with a simple stylised flower design similar to those painted on Scandinavian or American furniture. Again it is sufficiently simple for a beginner in cross stitch to attempt.

Aida Plus

In addition to fine evenweave fabrics such as Jobelan, we shall also be using Aida Plus in this chapter. Aida Plus is a 14-count Aida fabric already backed with a fine material, which prevents it fraying when cut into shapes. However, the stitching also shows on the back unless you add another backing, and this may not be suitable for your particular project. The Aida Plus is nevertheless ideal for unusually-shaped projects, where the back of the embroidery does not show – for example, key fobs backed in the same material, finger puppets, surrounds for pictures and photograph frames and three-dimensional decorations. It worked very well for

my material key fob, where I wanted to cut a heart shape and could add another backing, but was not suitable for the designs that I wanted to put into plastic fobs.

Aida Plus is available in a wide variety of colours. I chose the sage-green for my check heart because it blended best with the other colours I wanted to use. With Aida Plus, you can design any shape of key fob you wish. A star would be a challenge!

SAMPLER

**The finished sampler measures
29cm x 29cm (11½in x 11½in)**

YOU WILL NEED
*28-count grey Jobelan fabric,
46cm x 30cm (18in x 12in)
Light-coloured lining fabric, 46cm x 30cm (18in x 12in)
Iron-on interfacing, 46cm x 30cm (18in x 12in)
Stranded embroidery cotton as given in the key
No 24 tapestry needle
Pair of dark brown bell-pull rods, 20cm (8in)*

This project has been stitched in
Anchor six-stranded embroidery cotton

The Embroidery

1 Find the centre of your piece of fabric and the centre of your pattern. This is the best place to begin.
2 Use two strands of embroidery cotton in the needle and work over two threads of the material.
3 Steam press your embroidery on the wrong side when complete.

Finishing the Sampler

1 Centre the interfacing on the back of the embroidery and iron into position.
2 Trim the side edges until the backed embroidery measures 24cm (9½in) across. Make sure that the margins along each side of the embroidery are of

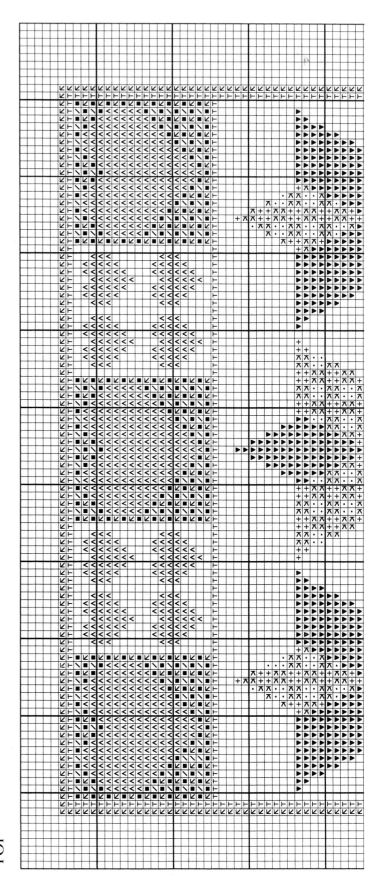

TOP

SAMPLER

		ANCHOR	DMC	MADEIRA
I	Brown	365	780	2302
−	Yellow	298	972	0106
+	Navy	150	823	1008
⌐	Dark blue	147	312	0912
·	Pale blue	120	800	0907
▼	Blue	145	334	0910
⊠	Light maroon	20	498	0511
⊥	Pink	893	224	0813
∧	Red	19	817	0211
∕	Pale green	259	772	1604
T	Light green	265	3348	1409
◹	Dark green	269	936	1507
▪	Green	267	470	1502
	Backstitch			
	Mouths	19	817	0211
	Faces			
	[dark grey]	400	414	1801

BOTTOM

even width. Turn in the side edges of the embroidery by 19mm (³/₄in) and press.

3 Trim the lining fabric to the same width and turn in along the side edges. Baste the lining fabric so that it covers the raw edges of the backed embroidery and comes to within 12mm (¹/₂in) of the side edge of the embroidery. Neatly slipstitch into position.

4 Trim the top and bottom of the embroidery so that it measures 34cm (13¹/₂in), this time making sure that the margins along the top and bottom of the embroidery are of equal depth.

5 Along the top and bottom edges of the embroidery, make a 6mm (¹/₄in) turning. Make a second 19mm (³/₄in) turning, taking the fabric over a rod at the top and bottom. Baste, and then neatly slipstitch in place.

KEY BOX

		ANCHOR	DMC	MADEIRA
⊞	Navy	150	823	1008
⊠	Dark blue	147	312	0912
⊡	Pale blue	120	800	0907
⊠	Bright blue	146	798	0911
↑	Blue	145	334	0910
⊟	Silver metallic thread			

KEY BOX

The finished key box measures
31.5cm x 26.5cm (12¹/₂in x 10¹/₂in)
and the oval aperture
18.5cm x 13.5cm (7¹/₄in x 5¹/₄in)

YOU WILL NEED
28-count forget-me-not pale blue Jobelan fabric,
28cm x 23cm (11in x 9in)
Iron-on interfacing, 28cm x 23cm (11in x 9in)
Stranded embroidery cotton as given in the key
No 24 tapestry needle
Wall-mounted key box (see list of suppliers at back of book)

This project has been stitched in
Anchor six-stranded embroidery cotton and
Anchor silver metallic thread

The Embroidery

1 Find the centre of your piece of Jobelan, and find the centre of your key box pattern.

2 Begin stitching at this point, using two strands of embroidery cotton in the needle and working over two threads of the Jobelan.

3 Gently steam press on the wrong side when complete.

Finishing the Key Box

1 Iron the piece of interfacing on to the back of the embroidery. This will help to keep it rigid and prevent it from wrinkling after insertion into the key box.

2 Insert the embroidery into the aperture of the box, according to the manufacturer's instructions.

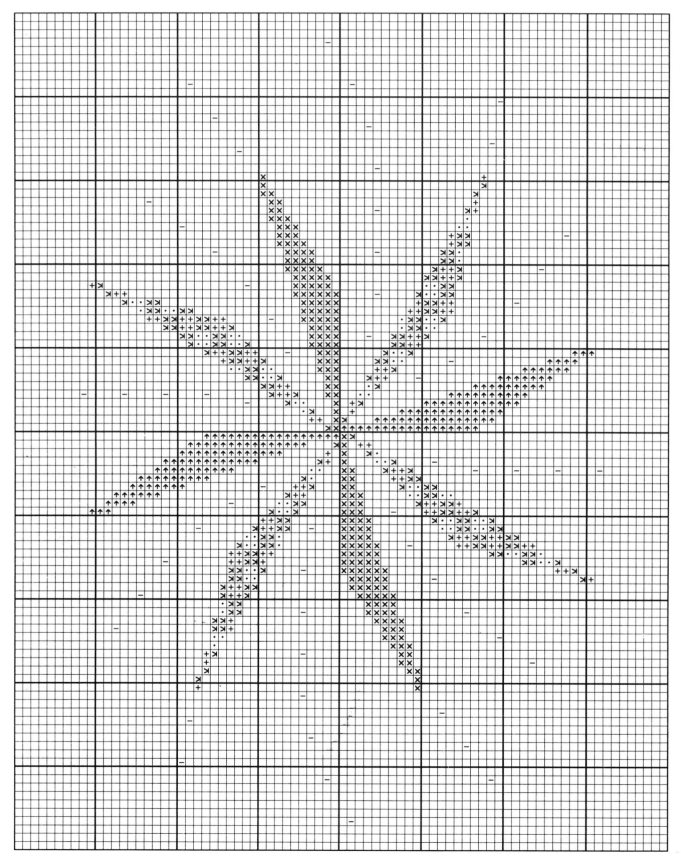

PLASTIC KEY FOB

The finished plastic key fob measures
6.5cm x 4.5cm (2¹/₂in x 1³/₄in)

YOU WILL NEED
28-count grey Jobelan fabric,
7.5cm x 7.5cm (3in x 3in)
Iron-on interfacing, 7.5cm x 7.5cm (3in x 3in)
Stranded embroidery cotton as given in the key
No 24 tapestry needle
Magnifying glass (optional)
Plastic key fob of the appropriate size

This project has been stitched in
Anchor six-stranded embroidery cotton

The Embroidery

1 Find the centre of the material, and then find the centre of your pattern.
2 Begin your embroidery from this point, using two strands of embroidery cotton in the needle, and working over two threads of the fabric.
3 When complete, steam press the work on the wrong side.

Finishing the Plastic Key Fob

1 Iron the interfacing on to the wrong side.
2 Using the clear plastic backing plate as a template, trim the material so that it just fits into the key fob. Take special care that the check embroidery goes right to the edge of the available space. Trim particularly carefully, so there is just one thread of material left around the edge. If necessary, use a magnifying glass for this operation! As long as you have ironed down the interfacing right to the edge, it should hold until you have your little embroidery safely inserted into the protective plastic fob.
3 Insert the embroidery into the plastic key fob.

PLASTIC LUGGAGE TAG

The finished plastic luggage tag measures
9.5cm x 6cm (3³/₄in x 2¹/₄in)

YOU WILL NEED
28-count grey Jobelan fabric,
11.5cm x 9cm (4¹/₂in x 3¹/₂in)
Iron-on interfacing, 11.5cm x 9cm (4¹/₂in x 3¹/₂in)
Stranded embroidery cotton as given in the key
No 24 tapestry needle
Plastic luggage tag of the appropriate size

This project has been stitched in
Anchor six-stranded embroidery cotton

The Embroidery

1 Find the centre of the material, and then find the centre of your pattern.
2 Begin your embroidery from this point, using two strands of embroidery cotton in the needle, and working over two threads of the fabric.
3 When complete, steam press the embroidery on the wrong side.

Finishing the Plastic Luggage Tag

1 Iron the interfacing on to the wrong side.
2 Using the clear plastic backing plate as a template, trim the material so that it just fits into the luggage tag.
3 Insert the embroidery into the protective plastic tag.

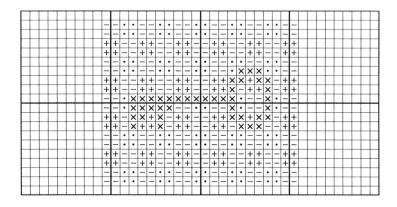

PLASTIC KEY FOB

		ANCHOR	DMC	MADEIRA
☒	Yellow	290	973	0105
＋	Navy	150	823	1008
－	Deep blue	147	312	0912
·	Pale blue	120	800	0907

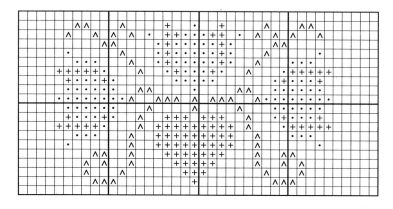

PLASTIC LUGGAGE TAG

		ANCHOR	DMC	MADEIRA
＋	Maroon	22	814	0514
·	Red	19	817	0211
∧	Green	267	470	1502

MATERIAL KEY FOB

		ANCHOR	DMC	MADEIRA
－	Green	267	470	1502
·	Pale green	259	772	1604
＋	Dark green	269	936	1507

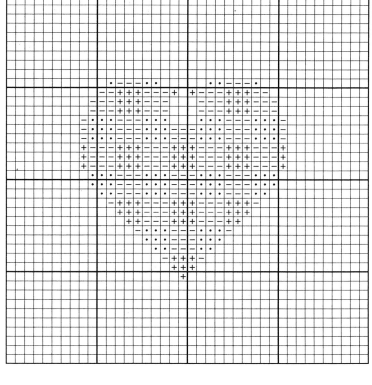

46

MATERIAL KEY FOB

The finished material key fob measures
4.5cm x 4.5cm (1³/₄in x 1³/₄in)

YOU WILL NEED
Two pieces of sage-green Aida Plus fabric,
7.5cm x 7.5cm (3in x 3in)
Stranded embroidery cotton as given in the key
No 24 tapestry needle
Sharp HB pencil
Thin card

This project has been stitched in
Anchor six-stranded embroidery cotton

The Embroidery

1 Find the centre of one of the pieces of Aida Plus fabric, and the centre point of your pattern. Begin stitching at this point.

2 When the stitching is complete, steam press the work on the wrong side.

3 Draw in the smooth shape of a heart, using the pencil and trim the fabric around this guide line.

Finishing the Material Key Fob

1 From the other piece of Aida Plus, cut a backing for your embroidery. If you wish to make it into a label, cut out a hole, 13 squares by 5 squares, from the middle of the backing heart. Cut a small piece of thin card a little larger than this aperture and stick it behind the opening. Alternatively, you may want to embroider both the front and back heart of the key fob.

2 Complete by sticking the embroidered heart and the backing heart back to back. You may have to trim the edges with scissors, to make them match exactly.

DESIGN TECHNIQUE FOR ANGLES

*V*ery often, you need to stitch lines at different angles to one another. I had to do this for the stars in the sampler, where the correct angles for the diamonds were crucial. They would also be important for architectural designs and other objects where perspective is essential.

It is not difficult to arrange the stitches to create a line at a particular angle. On your graph paper, identify the start and end point of the line you want and, with a ruler, draw this lightly in place. Now arrange even groups of stitches progressively along this line.

The illustration below shows how by combining different numbers of stitches you can create lines at different angles.

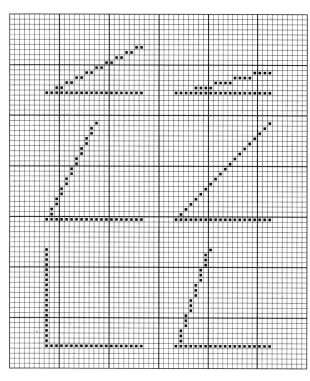

Forming angles in cross stitch

DRAWING AN OVAL SHAPE

YOU WILL NEED
Graph paper, 10 squares to the 2.5cm (1in)
Sharp HB pencil
Soft eraser
Coloured crayons
Measuring tape or ruler

Design Techniques

1 Before establishing your working area for an oval shape, you must first calculate the number of squares occupied by the shape on graph paper.

2 Measure your oval shape at its maximum width and multiply the measurement in inches by the count of your material. For example if the measurement across is 15cm (6in) and the count of material is 14, your pattern can be 6 x 14 = 84 squares across.

3 Then measure your oval shape at its maximum height and multiply the measurement in inches by the count of your material. For example, if the vertical measurement is 10cm (4in) and the count of your material is 14, your pattern can be 4 x 14 = 56 squares down.

4 On your graph paper, mark out an oblong 84 squares across by 56 squares down, with the pencil.

5 Within this rectangle draw an oval, using smooth lines to connect the centre point along the top line to the centre point of each side, and the centre point along the bottom line to the centre point of each side.

For designs such as the one I have done for the key box, the above method of establishing your working area for an oval shape is perfectly adequate. However, if you are intending to do a border following closely the curve of the oval, you will find a more accurate delimitation of the oval is necessary. In this case you should do calculations at several points both horizontally and vertically – for example horizontally at a quarter and at three-quarters of the way up the vertical line, and similarly in the other direction.

DESIGNING CHECKS

It is simple to design checks in cross stitch once you have decided on the colour you wish to use. Contrasting colours are important if the design is to stand out, and it is best if you choose three shades of the same colour – a dark, medium and very light shade. Then you need to decide on the size of the checks – is each block going to fill one square, four by four squares, nine by nine squares, 12 by 12 squares, or be even larger? The figure below may help to give you some ideas.

Checks in cross stitch

Another effective check design worth considering is to add stripes in backstitch to give a plaid effect.

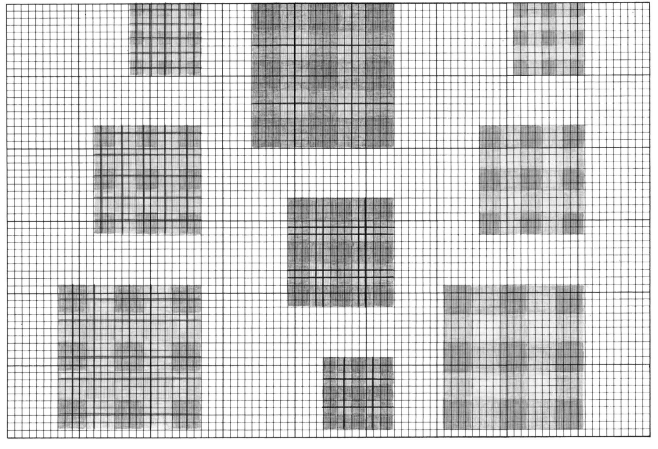

49

LEAFY INSPIRATION

*L*eaves are so lovely at all times of the year – the fresh green leaves of spring time, the great variety of greens in the mature leaves of summer, and especially the vast array of coloured leaves in autumn and early winter, but have you ever considered how many differently sized and shaped leaves there are? Leaves, large and small, play a very important part in decorative design work – on wallpaper, household furnishings, tiles, tableware, china and many other items around the home.

You can create your own designs in embroidery by taking your inspiration from something you are very fond of, as I did with my china tea service. Alternatively you could look at nature and use leaves collected on a walk in the countryside, or even a stroll around your own garden or local park. Ivy leaves are always a good shape to begin with, and their trailing stems and curling shoots add life and movement to any design. Particular favourites of mine are maple leaves. Their intricate shapes and spectacular autumn colours make them especially attractive subjects for cross stitch.

My special tea service is made by Royal Doulton, and is very prettily decorated with the Larchmont pattern. The leaves, in their dark olive-green and yellow shades, exude a touch of autumn, but what gives them such a delicate ethereal quality is the leaf shadows, cast in a soft blue-grey against the white china. I thought how pleasant it would be to sit on a comfortable chair, drinking tea from one of these pretty cups whilst resting my feet on a footstool decorated with a design to match my tea set. As I worked on my embroidery, my scissors, threads and needles would lie in a matching thread box beside me. Well, we can dream – but why not make the dream come true?

FOOTSTOOL

The finished footstool measures 23cm (9in) in diameter

YOU WILL NEED
28-count light grey Jobelan fabric,
52cm x 52cm (20½in x 20½in)
Stranded embroidery cotton as given in the key
Strong thread for lacing
No 24 tapestry needle
Sharp HB pencil
Footstool of your choice
(see list of suppliers at back of book)

This project has been stitched in
Madeira six-stranded embroidery cotton

NOTE Many footstools are made to take both embroidery on Jobelan, Aida, linen and similar materials, as well as fine tapestry canvas. You may find that a little padding is needed when mounting embroidery on finer materials, to make them fit flush against the wood at the edge.

The Embroidery

1 Find the centre of your piece of Jobelan fabric and mark with basting stitches.

2 Find the centre of your pattern and mark with the pencil.

3 Count to the nearest cross stitch. Finding the appropriate place to begin stitching on the material requires very careful counting of threads – remember that you will be working over two threads, so there will be two threads for each square on the pattern.

4 Work the design with two strands of embroidery cotton in the needle for the cross stitches, tall cross stitches and backstitches.

5 Trim the completed embroidery to shape, leaving 5cm (2in) turning under the footstool pad.

6 Steam press your embroidery on the wrong side.

Finishing the Footstool

1 Place your embroidery over the footstool pad so that your basting stitches marking the centre of the embroidery lie at the mid-point of the

Tall Cross Stitch

Tall cross stitches are worked across two threads in one direction and one thread in the other, and they therefore take up half the space occupied by a whole cross stitch.

Tall cross stitches can cover the top half, lower half, left- or right-hand side of a square on the pattern. When you get accustomed to them, they can be worked as quickly as full-sized cross stitches. Tall cross stitches have to be embroidered on linen, Jobelan, or similar material where the full-sized cross stitches are sewn over two fabric threads.

Although tall cross stitch is not very widely used in the United Kingdom, it is very popular in Denmark, especially in Danish botanical designs. It is often difficult to design leaves and flowers successfully using standard cross stitches, because stems and leaf veins may look out of proportion to the leaves and flowers. Full-sized cross stitches may be too wide and clumsy, and backstitch is too light, thin and spindly to be effective. Tall cross stitch provides a happy medium between the other two types of stitch.

The footstool will give you just a taste of using tall cross stitch in a simple way – for the leaf stalk of the bigger leaf, where the thickness of the

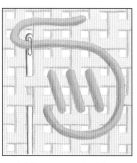

Tall cross stitch (a)

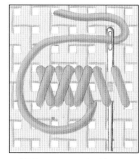

Tall cross stitch (b)

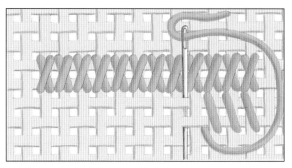

Tall cross stitch (c)

stitch is just right. In a later chapter (A Feast of Fruit), we shall be using the stitch more extensively, to make the fruit rounder, and in the leaf veins.

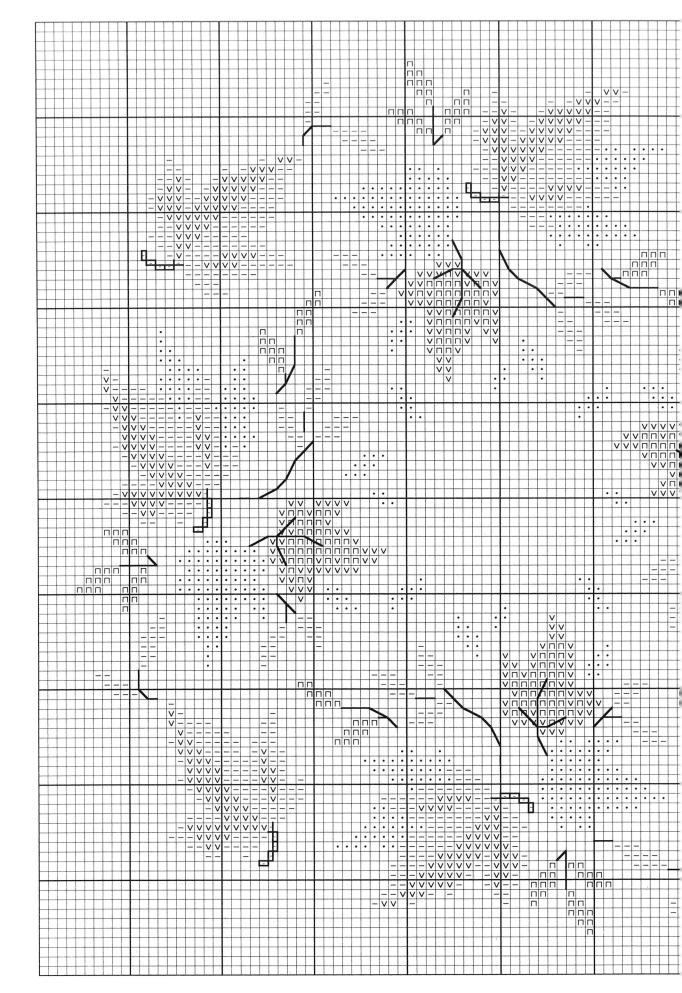

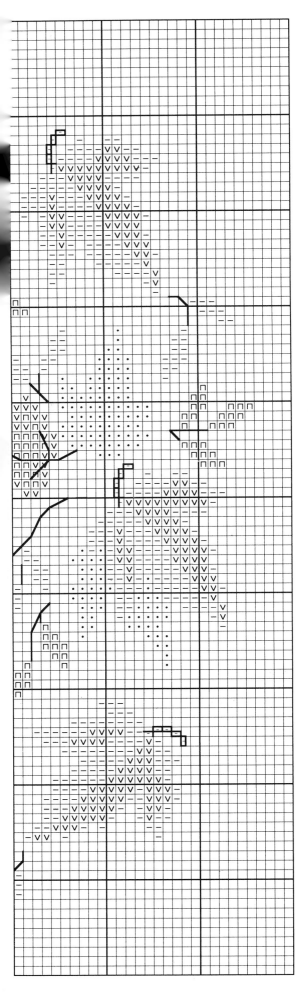

footstool pad. Use pins to hold your embroidery in place.

2 Turn your footstool pad over and, arranging the fullness of material evenly around it, lace the material round in a circular motion, easing it to fit smoothly over the pad as you go.

3 Press the edge of the footstool with a steam iron to remove any small folds or creases in your Jobelan.

FOOTSTOOL

		MADEIRA	DMC	ANCHOR
•	Blue-grey	1708	927	849
−	Dark green	1506	934	862
V	Light green	1509	3052	859
⊓	Orange	0114	742	303

Backstitch

Stalk and veins of all leaves except:	1506	934	862
Stalks of small yellow leaves	1509	3052	859

Long stitch

| Stalk of large leaf | 1506 | 934 | 862 |

THREAD BOX

		MADEIRA	DMC	ANCHOR
⊡	Blue-grey	1708	927	849
⊟	Dark green	1506	934	862
☑	Light green	1509	3052	859
⊓	Orange	0114	742	303

Backstitch

	MADEIRA	DMC	ANCHOR
Stalk and veins of all leaves except:	1506	934	862
Stalks of small yellow leaves	1509	3052	859

Long stitch

	MADEIRA	DMC	ANCHOR
Stalk of large leaf	1506	934	862

THREAD BOX

The finished thread box measures
11.5cm (4¹/₂in) in diameter

YOU WILL NEED
28-count light grey Jobelan fabric,
25cm x 25cm (10in x 10in)
Stranded embroidery cotton as given in the key
Strong thread for lacing
No 24 tapestry needle
Box with a padded top, to match your footstool
(see list of suppliers at back of book)

This project has been stitched in
Madeira six-stranded embroidery cotton

The Embroidery

1 Find the centre of your pattern, and the centre of your piece of fabric. This is the best place to begin.

2 Work the design over two threads of the fabric, using two strands of embroidery cotton in the needle for the cross stitches, tall cross stitches and backstitches.

3 When you have completed your embroidery, steam press on the wrong side.

Finishing the Thread Box

1 Centre your embroidery over the box pad, and lace it over in a circular direction, easing the material to fit smoothly over the pad as you go.

2 Press the edge of the pad with a steam iron to remove any small folds or creases in your material.

3 Screw the pad back into the box lid to complete.

NOTE Dark lines have been used on the chart to highlight the position of tall cross stitches, which occur on the large leaf stalks. These should not be confused with the backstitches.

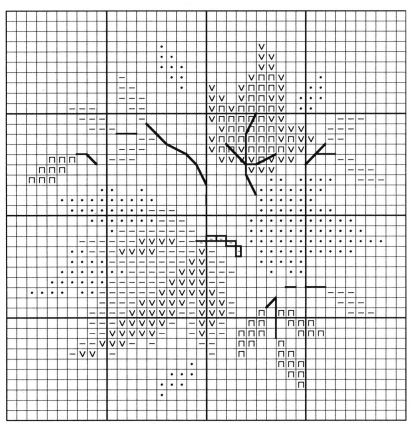

DESIGNING LEAVES

*L*eaves are almost two dimensional, and that is what makes them such an ideal subject for the beginner. Making leaves overlap, with lighter leaves overlaying darker ones, adds an extra dimension if you prefer.

Although leaves are all about us, when you decide to create a design with them you can be certain that the ones you want will be out of season! I therefore collect leaves year-round. In spring there are all the fresh green ones, small and perfectly formed. As spring gives way to summer, they become darker, and develop all sorts of imperfections brought about by weather and insects. By the time autumn approaches the riot of coloured leaves is spectacular.

When you begin collecting leaves you will be amazed not only by the variety of colours – even the different greens in spring – but also by the enormous contrasts in shape and size – even from the same tree. Your collection can also be increased by gathering from shrubs and herbaceous plants – but avoid flowers, which are likely to be a disappointment, as they lose their shape, form and much of their colour when pressed. Leaves, however, survive the process with much less damage, especially when positioned between sheets of newspaper, under heavy books. Stored safely there, you will have a resource for your designing, available at any time of the year.

The alternative, for those of you with access to a camera, is to take photographs. These are more convenient to store and the leaves never fade!

FROM LEAF TO CROSS STITCH PATTERN

YOU WILL NEED
2 pieces plain white paper
Transparent graph paper, 10 squares to the 2.5cm (1in),
large enough to accommodate the number of motifs
you wish to design
Graph paper, 10 squares to the 2.5cm (1in), large enough to
accommodate the number of motifs
you wish to design
Sharp HB pencil
Soft eraser
Coloured crayons
Masking tape
Leafy inspirational material
Manufacturer's shade card

1 Select the leaves that reflect or blend best with the leaves on your china or furnishing fabric, and arrange these on a piece of plain paper as you want them to look on your finished embroidery. Larger leaves look best towards the bottom of the design, with the smaller, more delicate ones sweeping up towards the top. If you have not tried designing before, you may wish to restrict yourself to individual leaves. Should you feel more confident, and if your design demands it, by overlapping the leaves you can get some beautiful results.

2 With the sharp pencil, draw around each leaf. Always begin at the bottom of the design, and remove each leaf as you finish drawing around it, to avoid damage. Go over your outlines with a firm line, and then, with the leaves in front of you, add the prominent leaf veins, leaf stalks and any colour changes you notice on each leaf.

3 Place a piece of transparent graph paper over your leaf outlines and secure it with masking tape. Moving only along the vertical and horizontal lines of the graph paper, follow as closely as possible the outlines of your leaf shapes. In the

Tracing over original leaf outline

same way, add lines to define areas of different colour.

4 Add the leaf veins and stalks. For large leaves these may be done in tall cross stitch. For smaller delicate leaves, the leaf veins can be worked in backstitch. Draw the veins and stalks as vertical or horizontal straight lines, or diagonal ones across single or double squares of the graph paper.

5 Detach your transparent graph paper from your paper with the leaf outlines, and place it over a fresh piece of plain paper, so that you can see your lines clearly. Make any adjustments if you feel they are necessary.

6 Transfer your blocked outline on to a piece of ordinary graph paper. Note any backstitch and add leaf colours with crayons or symbols.

7 Using your manufacturer's shade card, select the colours for your leaves. Shades often look darker when worked than in the skein, and it is wise to choose a slightly lighter colour than that of the leaf itself to avoid your delicate leaves looking garish and heavy. Also remember that the colours of a leaf change subtly and almost

imperceptibly across its surface. To achieve such an effect requires patience and considerable experimentation.

8 If you are ambitious, you could add leaf shadows, to throw the main leaves forward and give depth to your design. To do this, draw a second leaf of a similar shape to the first, just to one side of the original, and at a slight angle. The second leaf requires no shading, no veins or stalk, and it would look well in some pastel shade of blue-grey.

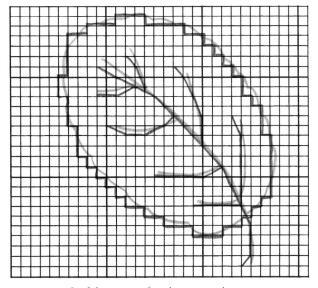

Leaf design transferred on to graph paper

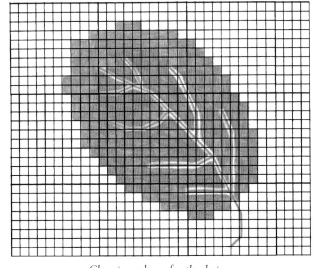

Choosing colours for the design

DESIGNING WITH CIRCLES

The easiest way to design embroidery within a circle is to create one motif and then repeat it around the circle, filling in any spaces with leaves for example.

YOU WILL NEED

Graph paper, 10 squares to the 2.5cm (1in), large enough to accommodate the number of motifs you wish to design
Sharp HB pencil
Soft eraser
Coloured crayons
Paper scissors
Compass
Ruler
Paper glue

Design Techniques

Small circular designs

1 To create a small motif on a circular object with a diameter of 11.5cm (4½in), you will need no more than 36 stitches across, if working on 28-count fabric, stitching over two threads.

2 On the graph paper, draw a 36 by 36 square block in which to draw your own leaf design. This will be the approximate size of your chart. Find the centre point and mark clearly.

3 Using the compass, put the point into the centre of your chart and draw a circle just touching the square at the middle point of each side. This circle represents the area that you can cover with embroidery without your embroidery coming too close to the edge of the circular object.

4 Use bold lines to create your leaf design.

5 When you are satisfied, go over each of the main lines again, this time following the horizontal and vertical lines of the graph paper as closely as possible.

6 Use differently coloured crayons or symbols to show the individual colours on the leaf design.

7 Complete with a key.

8 Try out your small motif on a piece of 28-count material.

Larger circular designs

For a circular object with a diameter of 23cm (9in), your design should need no more than a 92 by 92 square block. You can use the same design as for the smaller-diameter object, this time creating a repeat pattern, going in a circular fashion.

1 Make four photocopies of your pattern created for the small circular design and cut them out, so that there is no space on any of the four sides of the chart.

2 Cut out a 90 by 90 square block of graph paper. Using the compass, draw a circle just touching the square edges, then with the ruler divide your circle into quadrants.

3 Place the centre of one of the photocopies of your leaf motif along one of these lines, so that the top of the design is 11 squares from the centre point. It must be placed so that the line bisects the design exactly. Paste it in place.

4 Turn your circle 90 degrees clockwise, and taking another of the photocopies of your design, paste it 11 squares from the centre point and on the line, so that the line bisects the design, as with the first motif.

5 Continue this process twice more, and you should have your motifs spaced equidistant in your circle.

6 Add further leaves to fill the space between two of the motifs, in order to achieve a more circular appearance to the pattern.

7 Then rotating your pattern by 90 degrees each time, add the extra leaves in the three other spaces between motifs. Your design should now be ready for stitching . . . so collect up your needle and threads, and try it out!

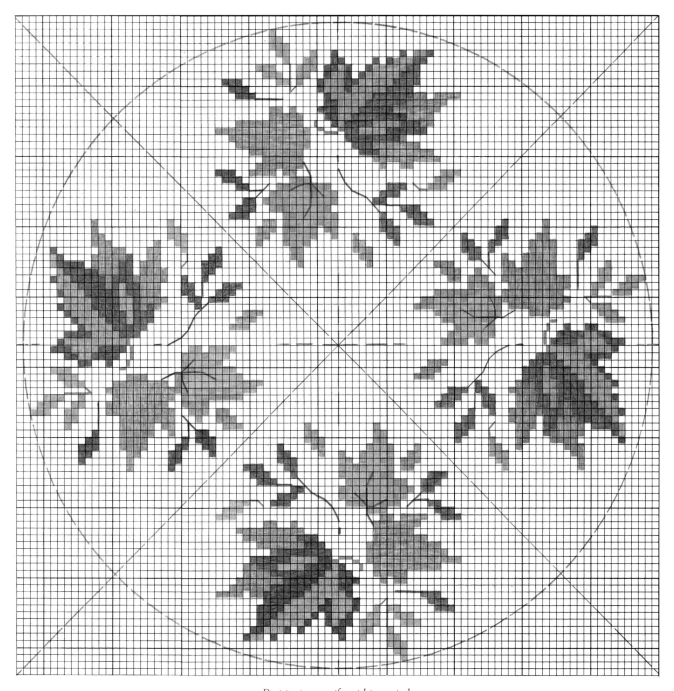

Positioning motifs within a circle

SINGLE-COLOUR THEMES

Blue has always been my favourite colour, so perhaps this partly explains my fascination with Delftware – the attractive, blue-and-white ceramic ware that comes from the world-renowned Dutch town of Delft. The challenge of creating a pleasing picture, using only shades of blue, appealed to me. As blue is so popular for kitchens, I enthusiastically began to design projects that would look quite at home in many kitchens.

Many of the Delftware designs inevitably include a windmill – an image inextricably linked with Holland. My thoughts then moved on from Holland to my own native Lincolnshire – another region associated with the windmill. Here it was employed in grinding corn and, in the south, in draining the fenlands. Though I have lived for most of my life in the English Midlands, Lincolnshire is still my spiritual home, and where my roots are, and so I determined that the mills I chose for my designs should all be from that county.

Windmills have existed in western Europe since the twelfth century, and since that time they have taken on a variety of different shapes and forms – the older post mills were followed by the tower mills and smock mills. Typical of Lincolnshire are the tower mills, built of durable materials like bricks and masonry, and standing up to 27m (90ft)

high. A covering of tar was often used to weatherproof the brickwork. Towers typically tapered towards the top to make them more stable and to reduce wind resistance immediately behind the sails. The number of sails varied, some having four, some five, some six and a few had eight. The rotating cap, carrying the sails of the mill and used to turn the sails into the wind, was built of timber and often painted white. Typical Lincolnshire mills had caps shaped like a Turk's headgear, and topped by a ball finial.

For the single-colour projects in this chapter, I chose three Lincolnshire windmills. Although in designs of this size it is impossible to include much detail, hopefully they are recognisable to those of you who may know them.

On the apron pocket I have reproduced Heckington mill – the only eight-sailed windmill left in England. Built in 1830, it originally had only six sails, with which it worked for 40 years. It then suffered horrendous damage by fire and strong winds. Heckington mill was then purchased and repaired by John Pocklington, who also bought another mill in Boston, which was due to be demolished. The cap, sails, fantail and all the interior workings were brought up from the Boston mill and fitted in the Heckington body. By the mid 1890s the mill

was working again, grinding corn and also driving a circular saw that cut elm boards to make coffins for the village. It finally ceased work in 1943, but has since been repaired and renovated by the council. It stands as a proud monument to the age of wind power.

One of the two designs on the basket cloth is of Alford mill. Until 1931 Alford had four-, five- and six-sailed windmills working in the town. This five-sailed windmill, built by a local man in 1837, is the only one to survive. It has six floors and is approximately 18m (60ft) high. The second windmill design on the basket cloth is of Trader mill. This 23m (75ft) high mill was built in Sibsey in 1877 on the site of an old post mill. It was a working mill until the 1950s, by which time it had only four sails. In 1970 it was fully restored with two new sails, a repaired cap and replaced bricks in the tower. Unlike the other two mills I have featured in this chapter, the brickwork of Trader mill is exposed. It also has an elegant, wrought-iron stage around it, but sadly on the scale of my designs I am unable to show this.

Salisbury Fabric

This fine 30-count evenweave material combines the texture of linen with the softness of cotton: it is made of 60 per cent linen and 40 per cent cotton. Salisbury is best worked over two threads, thus making it the equivalent of a 15-count fabric. However, it differs from Jobelan in that the fabric threads are not of even thickness, which means that, as with a linen, special care must be taken when counting the threads to avoid overlooking one. This attractive material is available in white, cream, blue, yellow, beige, rose and green.

BASKET CLOTH

The finished basket cloth measures
31.5cm x 31.5cm (12^1/$_2$in x 12^1/$_2$in)

YOU WILL NEED
30-count blue Salisbury fabric, 38cm x 38cm (15in x 15in)
Stranded embroidery cotton as given in the key
Matching sewing cotton
No 24 tapestry needle

This project has been stitched in
Madeira six-stranded embroidery cotton

The Embroidery

1 Using a light-coloured sewing cotton, run a line of basting stitches all the way around your cloth, 3cm (1^1/$_4$in) from the edge of the material.

2 Measure in 2.5cm (1in) from this line and do a second line of basting stitches inside the first row to mark out your border. Your second row of basting stitches gives you the position of the right-hand edge and the bottom edge of your design.

3 Fit one windmill into each of the four corners, alternating Alford mill with Trader mill and rotating them at 90 degrees to one another.

4 Find the centre of the pattern you are going to start with.

5 Stitch the designs over two threads of the material, using two strands of embroidery cotton in the needle. Be careful when counting the threads in from the right side of the base line to find the centre point for your design. Remember that you should allow two strands for each stitch! Also, Salisbury has threads that vary in thickness; be careful not to overlook some of the finer ones when counting.

6 Complete all the cross stitch first, and then the backstitch.

7 When you have completed all four windmills, steam press your work on the wrong side.

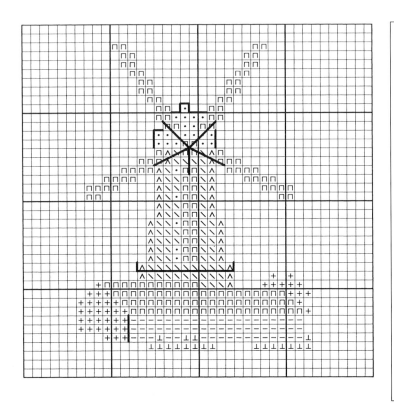

BASKET CLOTH:
ALFORD MILL

		MADEIRA	DMC	ANCHOR
·	White	White	Blanc	White
◲	Navy	1007	336	150
+	Light navy	1005	312	979
⊓	Light blue	0910	334	145
−	Pale blue	0908	800	128
∧	Dark navy	1008	823	152
⊥	Deep blue	0912	797	132

Backstitch

Walkway around mill and shed	White	Blanc	White
Sails and cap of windmill	1005	312	979

BASKET CLOTH:
TRADER MILL

		MADEIRA	DMC	ANCHOR
·	White	White	Blanc	White
∧	Dark navy	1008	823	152
⊥	Deep blue	0912	797	132
Y	Blue	0911	798	131
+	Light navy	1005	312	979
⊓	Light blue	0910	334	145
−	Pale blue	0908	800	128
◲	Navy	1007	336	150

Backstitch

Sails and cap of windmill	1005	312	979
Balcony rail and door	White	Blanc	White
Walkway around windmill	1008	823	152

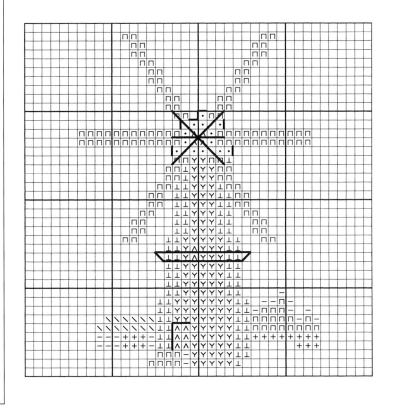

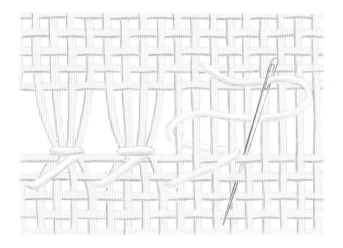

Hemstitch

Finishing the Cloth

1 Hemstitch a narrow hem on all sides of the cloth.

2 Remove one or two threads from the fabric near the hemline.

3 Bring the needle out on the right side, two threads below the drawn thread line.

4 Working from left to right, pick up two, three or four threads according to their thickness. The reason for varying the number of threads is to keep the resulting hemstitching even.

5 Bring the needle out again and insert it behind the fabric, to emerge two/three/four threads down, ready to make the next stitch.

6 Before reinserting the needle, pull the thread tight, so that the bound threads form a neat group.

APRON

The finished apron measures
81cm x 62.5cm (32in x 25in)
and the pocket 15cm x 17.5cm (6in x 7in)

YOU WILL NEED
Blue check gingham material, 1.25m x 1m (1¹/₂yd x 1yd)
28-count forget-me-not blue Jobelan fabric,
20cm x 24cm (8in x 9¹/₂in)
Stranded embroidery cotton as given in the key
Matching sewing cotton
No 24 tapestry needle

This project has been stitched in
Madeira six-stranded embroidery cotton

The Embroidery

1 Find the centre of the pattern for Heckington mill.

2 Find the centre of your piece of Jobelan fabric, and begin stitching at this point. I used three strands of embroidery cotton in the needle, as I wanted to achieve a solid effect. For a lighter result use only two strands, and you will be able to see the pale blue material through your dark cross stitches. It is up to you to decide upon the finish you want. Either way, the cross stitches are worked over two strands of the material.

3 Work all the cross stitches first, and then the backstitches.

4 Trim your embroidery until the Jobelan measures 23cm (9in) down by 17.5cm (7in) across.

5 When complete, steam press on the wrong side.

Finishing the Apron

1 Cut out the following pieces from the gingham material:

86cm x 64.5cm (34in x 25¹/₂in) for the apron;
60cm x 13cm (24in x 5in) for the waist band;
two pieces of 81cm x 10cm (32in x 4in) for the ties.

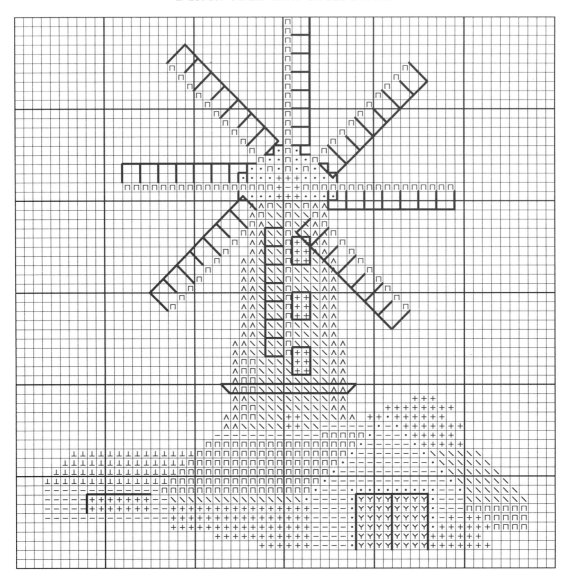

APRON POCKET: HECKINGTON MILL

		MADEIRA	DMC	ANCHOR
⊡	White	White	Blanc	White
⊥	Deep blue	0912	797	132
Y	Blue	0911	798	131
⊓	Light blue	0910	334	145
⊟	Pale blue	0908	800	128
⋀	Dark navy	1008	823	152
⟍	Navy	1007	336	150
⊞	Light navy	1005	312	979

Backstitch	MADEIRA	DMC	ANCHOR
Sails of windmill	0910	334	145
Cap of mill, shed window and doors	1008	823	152
Mill windows and walkway around windmill	White	Blanc	White

2 Make a narrow hem down each of the two shorter sides of the apron.

3 Make two rows of fine running stitches, one about 19mm (³/₄in) from the raw edge of one of the longer sides of the apron (to mark the line where the apron will be attached to the waist band), and a second row about 6mm (¹/₄in) above it.

4 Turn in one long edge of the waist band by 12mm (¹/₂in) and baste.

5 Find and mark the halves and quarters of both the gathered edge of the apron and the waist band, and then draw up the gathers so that they fit evenly against the waist band. Pin the gathered apron to the waist band so that the raw edges are together, and the gathers evenly distributed. Baste in position and then machine in place on the right side.

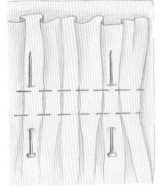

6 Turn the wrong side of the band over the gathers with the fold to the fitting line. Baste, and then hem neatly into position, taking care that your stitches do not go through to the right side of the waist band.

Pin the gathered apron to the waist band

7 Fold the two ties in half lengthways, right side in, and baste, taking a 12mm (¹/₂in) seam. Machine stitch the two ties, continuing your stitching around one end of each tie.

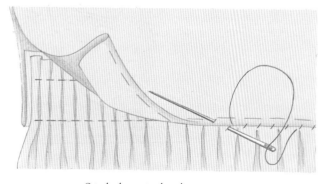

Stitch the waist band into position

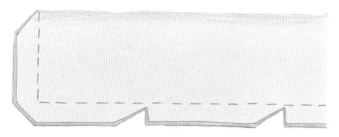

Trim the tie corners and clip the seam edges

8 Trim the corners of the ties and clip the seam edges at intervals.

9 Press the seam open and turn the ties right side out.

10 Press and then stitch neatly in place on either side of the waist band.

11 Turn up a 4cm (1¹/₂in) hem along the bottom of the apron and hem neatly.

12 Turn in the top of the pocket 4cm (1¹/₂in) and then take a 6mm (¹/₄in) turning, and hem neatly.

13 Press, and then, turning in the raw edges on the other three sides 12mm (¹/₂in), pin and baste the pocket in the correct position on the apron. Stitch into position.

ADAPTING THE DESIGNS

*T*hese blue-and-white windmills would look attractive on many different items. You could, for example, make other things for your kitchen. The larger windmill could be worked on a tea cosy, and you could design your own border to stitch around the edge. The smaller windmills would look good on egg cosies. Alternatively, why not stitch each windmill separately and frame them as a matching set of pictures? You can even add others of your own as you become more adventurous. Finally, why not sew a windmill on a birthday card to give to a windmill enthusiast?

Designing a Single-colour Image

I am sure you will have great fun dreaming up ideas to translate into single-colour designs. You may find suitable images on favourite tiles, china or fabrics that are already in different shades of the same colour and designing from these will help you develop an eye for how the shades work together. Alternatively, perhaps you have a special building or scene you would like to reproduce, a place that you have noticed or visited on holiday, or perhaps you would like to use something that is local to you. Unearth your photographs or take a new one and follow my suggestions. Remember that the larger the design, the more detail you can show, and the more realistic you can make it.

I like graph paper with ten squares to 2.5cm (1in) best, as it leaves plenty of room to put the coloured dots or symbols in when the design is complete. My design of Heckington mill was 58 squares down by 54 squares across. If you have already worked the design according to the instructions, you will know how big it comes out on 30-count material (the equivalent of 15 count when worked over two threads).

YOU WILL NEED
Graph paper, 10 squares to the 2.5cm (1in),
at least 58 by 54 squares in total
Sharp HB pencil
Soft eraser
Coloured crayons
Good clear photograph of your favourite image
Manufacturer's shade card

Design Techniques
1 From a clear photograph, make a drawing of your chosen image on your graph paper with the pencil. Use bold lines and avoid putting in details that you cannot hope to show on your embroidery. For example, on a windmill, it would be easier if the sails face towards you, as this avoids having to show the fantail and the complicated workings at the back. On the other hand you may welcome a challenge and opt to do your subject from a different angle.

2 Once you are satisfied with your design, redraw its main outlines following as closely as possible the vertical and horizontal lines of the graph paper. As you do this, erase your original sketch lines to avoid confusion.

3 Choose coloured crayons or symbols to identify the white and various shades of blue, or any other colour, you wish to use. Your choice of shades and how you incorporate them are important to ensure that the design is clear and does not become an unidentifiable blur of one colour.

4 I used eight shades (white and seven shades of blue), which I carefully chose from the manufacturer's shade card. It was my intention to try to keep as close as I could to traditional Delftware. You may find it helpful to photocopy your photograph. Seeing the image in black and white will help you to identify where the lightest and the darkest areas occur as well as the shades in between. Try not to choose shades that are too close together for areas where you want to define a shape, because close shades merge together and can look dull.

5 Keep the shapes as simple as possible, including just enough detail to be able to distinguish the main features of your subject. If you find further definition is needed, consider outlining some of the areas with a darker shade of backstitch.

6 Use my design for Heckington mill as a guide, but do not be afraid to experiment for yourself with other sources of inspiration.

7 When you are happy with your design, complete with a key.

SEA CREATURES FROM STENCILS

So far we have explored a wealth of ideas for making cross stitch both varied and interesting. I have created designs to decorate a host of familiar household articles, and worked them on diverse shapes and sizes. In this chapter I wanted to use some delightful stencils of marine creatures as a source of inspiration to create a design that gave my bathroom a very personal appeal. This resulted in a

design on a much larger scale than is usual for cross stitch. The mono canvas and tapisserie wool I used, together with a little imagination, gave me a bold and serviceable mat. To complement this, I embroidered a guest towel on a similar theme.

I chose the seahorse for my bathroom mat principally because the animal's lovely head with its large swivel eyes, its lithe elegant body and its sensitive prehensile tail

had an aesthetic appeal for me. Further, as a conservationist I was attracted to the seahorse by its current plight. Of the 35 or so species found world-wide, almost all are now endangered.

You will most certainly have your own favourite sea creatures. Whether they be dolphins, whales, penguins or fishes you will probably find appropriate stencils, but whatever the subject you favour, the approach and the skills are the same.

Having chosen the main topic for my design, the next decision was the nature of the border. My problem was solved when I visited the ancient Roman site of Verulamium, at St Albans. Around one of the mosaics was a simple wave design in brown and gold, representing incurving waves thundering up a beach. I have adapted this idea for the border of my bathroom mat. In a navy and a light blue, it acts as a suitable foil for the four sea-green seahorses.

The small colourful tropical fish was also inspired by a simple stencil shape. The black and gold of the fish against the soft blue towel appealed to me, and the towel matched the blue in the border of the bathroom mat almost exactly.

Mono Canvas

Mono or single-thread canvas is pleasant to work with, but it is advisable to bind the edges with masking tape before you start. This will prevent your wool from snagging on the edge of the canvas and avoid chafing your hands. It may also be worth using a thimble, even if you are not in the habit of using one. Cross stitch, worked in tapisserie wool on 10-count canvas, gives a very firm, hard-wearing finish. It can, however, be

tough on the fingers, especially when filling in a small space between areas already worked. Care needs to be taken when easing the wool through the holes, but the stitches will 'bed down'.

A tapestry needle is essential with mono canvas as its blunt end will not split the threads of the canvas or the wool you are working with. The long eye is easy to thread, and the threaded needle should pass through the holes of the canvas without tugging. As with any cross stitch, all stitches should be worked in the same way and all top stitches should lie in the same direction.

Embroidery Frames

When embroidering, the choice of whether or not you use a frame is a matter of personal preference. Cross stitch, where there is an even 'pull' on the fabric in each direction, should not cause diagonal distortion – unlike many stitches done on canvas. I stitched the bathroom mat without a frame, but I did need a small table beside me to take the weight of the mat in its later stages of working as it became too heavy to hold.

BATHROOM MAT

The finished bathroom mat measures 67cm x 46cm (26$\frac{1}{2}$in x 18in)

YOU WILL NEED
10-hole mono canvas, 81cm x 60cm (32in x 24in)
Strong blue backing fabric, 81cm x 60cm (32in x 24in)
Tapisserie wools as given in the key
No 18 or 24 tapestry needle

This project has been stitched in Anchor tapisserie wools

The Embroidery

1 Whether you begin in the middle of the pattern or with the border is up to you, but I would stress the need for careful counting, as with all cross

Section A

stitch. Unpicking wool is not only time consuming but is also very expensive!

2 Begin with a short 'tail' of wool at the back, and carefully secure this with your first half-dozen stitches. When you have come to the end of your wool, leave about 2.5cm (1in) at the back of your work and secure this as you begin stitching with your next needleful of wool.

3 Avoid working the background in blocks as the line along which you join the blocks will show up on the finished work, and the even 'ribbed' finish will be spoilt. You can turn your mat upside down to work, if convenient, but it is not advisable to turn it sideways, as this leads to mistakes in keeping the top thread going in the right direction.

The chart for the bathroom mat has been split over four pages. Refer to this diagram to check the relevant page on which each section of the chart falls

A	B
page 76	*page 77*
C	D
page 78	*page 79*

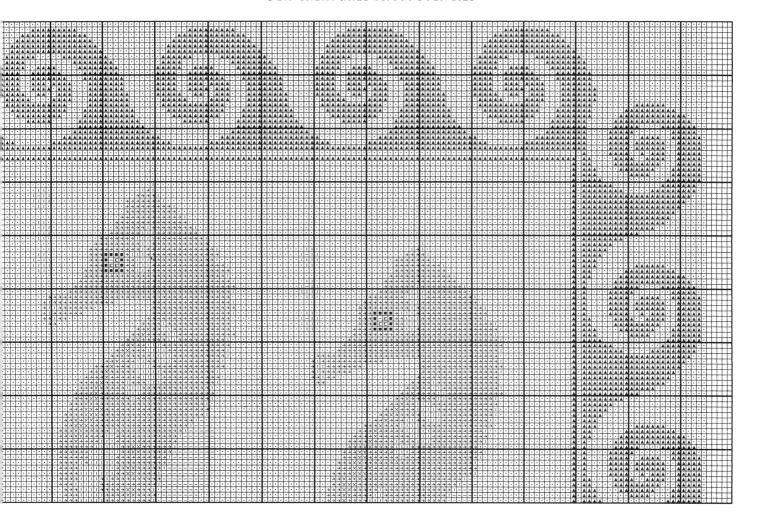

Section B

Finishing the Bathroom Mat

1 Trim the embroidered canvas, leaving 4cm (1½in) of canvas around the edge.

2 Carefully mitre the corners and fold back the canvas so that no unworked canvas shows from the front. With strong thread hold the canvas in place with basting stitches.

3 Working along the long sides first, turn the edges of the backing fabric in, and first baste and then hem firmly in place. During this process you must ensure that the mat remains flat.

4 Finally, trim and turn in the backing material along the two ends.

5 Steam press the backing fabric when complete.

BATHROOM MAT

		ANCHOR TAPISSERIE WOOL	DMC TAPESTRY WOOL	No of skeins
E	Black	9800	Noir	1
−	Ecru	8006	Ecru	1
■	Dusky yellow	8056	7472	1
Z	Sandy brown	8060	7455	1
•	Navy	8838	7288	50
▲	Light blue	8832	7594	20
I	Pale blue	8912	7599	2
→	Turquoise	8918	7598	10
X	Dark turquoise	8938	7596	1

Section C

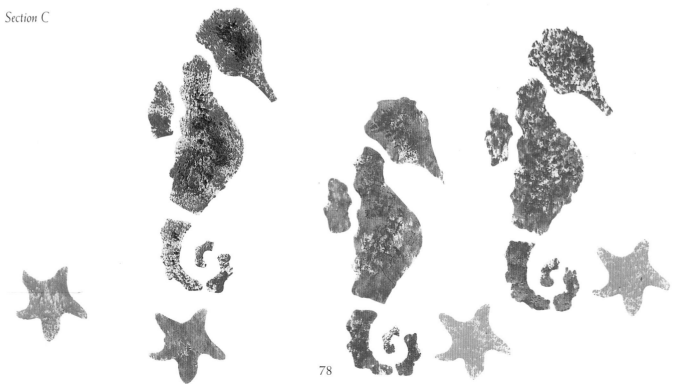

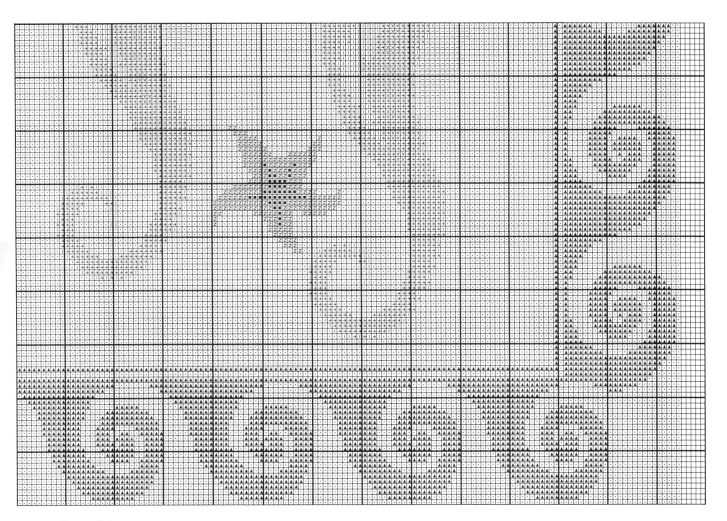

Section D

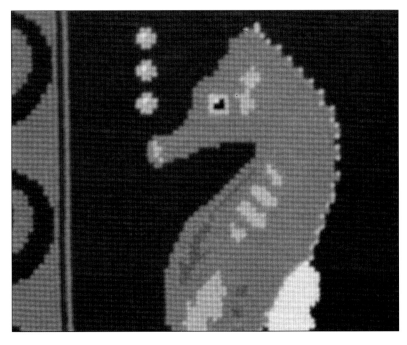

GUEST TOWEL

The finished guest towel measures
46cm x 29cm (18in x 11½in)

YOU WILL NEED

Small blue guest towel with 14-count evenweave inset
for embroidery
Stranded embroidery cotton as given in the key
No 24 tapestry needle

This project has been stitched in
Anchor six-stranded embroidery cotton

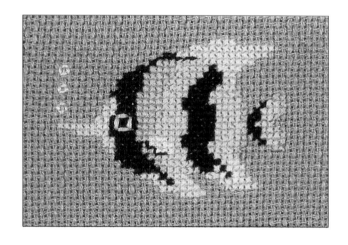

The Embroidery

1 Find the centre of your evenweave panel, and start your embroidery from the centre of the design.

2 Work all the cross stitches first, using three strands of embroidery cotton.

3 Then add the backstitching, using two strands for the bubbles and fins and three strands for the eye outlines.

4 Gently steam press the towel when complete. No further finishing is required.

GUEST TOWEL

		ANCHOR	DMC	MADEIRA
+	Black	403	310	Black
−	Cream	292	3078	0102
✕	Lemon	295	726	0109
T	Yellow	298	444	0105
↓	Deep yellow	303	741	0201
	Backstitch			
	Eye outline	298	444	0105
	Bubbles	292	3078	0102
	Fins	403	310	Black

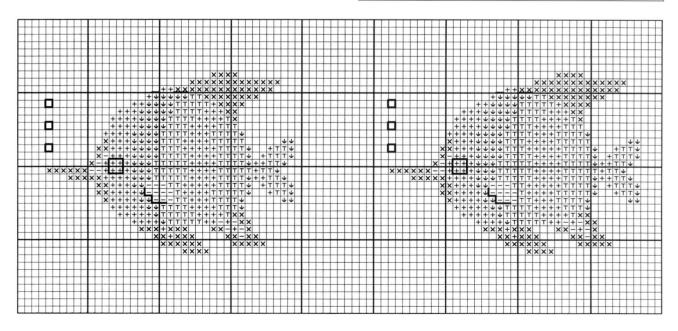

ADAPTING THESE DESIGNS

*I*f the colours that I have used do not fit your present décor, you can, using a manufacturer's shade card, select different ones for the same basic design. Should you feel a little more adventurous, you may wish to adapt my designs to make other matching items for your bathroom, or for other purposes. A couple of the seahorses with a modified border would make an eye-catching beach bag for your summer holidays. Leave the border off entirely and cut the shape of the canvas to fit your toilet seat, and you have a matching bathroom set.

Rather than putting the bathroom mat on the floor, you may prefer to hang it on the wall. If it is too large to display in this way, why not work the design on 28-count navy Jobelan fabric, stitched over two threads to make a smaller matching picture? On 22-count dark blue or navy Hardanger fabric, you might like to embroider a single seahorse on tie-backs for your bathroom curtains. To make a pair, reverse the design for the left-hand curtain – a tedious but simple procedure. Also, a seahorse on the same 22-count Hardanger could fit into a 5.5cm (2½in) door finger-plate. A little fish would tuck into a 7.5cm (3in) trinket bowl to hold small bathroom necessities, or fishes could be embroidered along a long strip to decorate and finish off the edge of a bathroom shelf. The possibilities are limited only by your imagination, and I am sure you will have many more ideas. If you are feeling brave, however, you may want to create your own design.

CREATING YOUR OWN BATHROOM MAT DESIGN

YOU WILL NEED
Graph paper, 10 squares to the 2.5cm (1in), at least 300 by 200 squares in total so that your pattern will be the exact size of your finished mat
Firm level surface to work on
Sharp HB pencil
Soft eraser
Coloured crayons
Manufacturer's shade card for tapisserie wools
Inspirational material, such as stencils matching those in your room, stencilled test pieces or any photographs or pictures to help fill in the detail of your chosen subject

Design Techniques

1 Decide upon the size of your bathroom mat. It is not necessary to be absolutely exact at this stage because the size will depend on the width of each repeat pattern of the border, but decide to the nearest 2.5cm (1in) either way. Remember that the bigger the mat the longer it is going to take to work – and when you remember that one complete row of the seahorse mat may take an hour and a half to complete, this is an important consideration!

2 If you require your mat to be the same size as the seahorse bathroom mat, draw a rectangle of 270 by 180 squares on your graph paper with the pencil.

3 Mark off an inner rectangle 25 squares in from the edge all the way round. This area represents the border.

4 Mark the centre point along the lower border on the graph paper, and the centre point along the left-hand border.

5 Beginning from either of these points, draw a simple motif or pattern.

6 When you are satisfied with it, carefully draw around the pencil outlines of your drawing, this

time following the horizontal and vertical lines of the grid.

7 If you are keeping to a two-colour border, you may find it easier to pencil or crayon in the squares to be stitched in the darker colour.

8 Working towards the left-hand bottom corner, repeat your motif until you reach within 25 squares of the left-hand edge of the mat.

9 Now repeat the process from the centre of the left-hand border. If you are lucky, you will find that both vertical and horizontal lines of motifs can be joined in the 25 by 25 square at the bottom left-hand corner. If not, you may need to adjust the width and length of your design.

10 If your motif is simple and symmetrical, repeat it as a mirror image in each of the four quarters of the border. If it is a more complex, flowing design, like the waves, you will need a lot more time and patience to work it out, but it will be very satisfying in the long run. One word of warning — avoid having a lot of different colours in small areas, which will be difficult to work and very hard on the fingers!

11 Using your favourite stencil to guide you, draw boldly, using clear simple lines, the outline of your sea creature. Make sure that it is positioned centrally. If there is more than one,

ensure that they are arranged exactly as you want them on your finished design.

12 Mark off areas of a different colour within your general outline, using any photographs or pictures you may have to guide you, but again avoid complex changes of colour. Aim to use no more than half a dozen different shades for your animal.

13 When you are happy with the design for your central panel, carefully draw around the lines, again following the horizontal and vertical lines of the grid. You will now have demarcated the basic areas of different colour in your design. Use the coloured crayons to shade these in or else devise symbols to represent each colour.

14 Using the manufacturer's shade card, decide upon the colours you wish to use. This is sometimes not as easy as it seems. Colours frequently look different in isolation from the way they appear when stitched adjacent to others in a design. For example the dark turquoise, used for shading on the seahorses, looks very bright when seen on its own, but when surrounded by the turquoise it appears much more mellow; so choose your colours carefully and be prepared to experiment.

15 Complete with a key.

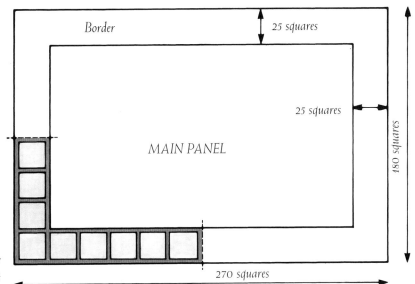

First stages in planning your design for a bathroom mat

Border

25 squares

25 squares

180 squares

MAIN PANEL

270 squares

A FEAST OF FRUIT

What more beautiful gift could anyone give to an enthusiastic cross stitcher than a length of Verona fabric? When I received a large piece of this very special material, soft and creamy in colour, I debated for a long time what I should use it for. It would have made a lovely Christmas table centre, be ideal for festive place settings, a cloth for a christening spread, for bar mitzvah items or for some special gift for a golden wedding celebration; but all these would have had limited use or restricted appeal.

I decided upon a tablecloth that could be used at any time, and I searched for inspiration amongst my tableware. I did not have to go far because my favourite dinner service is Royal Worcester Evesham Gold, which really looks superb when the table is set. The name conjures up pictures of the Vale of Evesham, one of Britain's most intensively cultivated areas. It lies astride the River Avon, to the south-east of the city of Worcester. Market gardening and fruit growing take place on traditional smallholdings. In spring the fruit blossom attracts tourists to the area and in summer and early autumn visitors flock there to pick their own fruit. Royal Worcester's Evesham Gold mirrors the traditional agriculture and 'mellow fruitfulness' of the Vale of Evesham.

Perhaps it is my familiarity with the area,

maybe it is the realistic studies of the fruit portrayed on the tableware, or possibly it is the rich colours that appeal to me. Suffice it to say, as I mulled over the idea, I knew that not only would the fruit on the tableware be the inspiration for my tablecloth design but also that the two would complement each other perfectly.

Verona is a 28-count evenweave fabric made from 60 per cent rayon and 40 per cent cotton. It is divided into 7.5cm (3in) squares, which are separated by a double row of running stitches in gold metallic thread. Even the gold edging of the Evesham Gold tableware is reflected in the gold metallic threads.

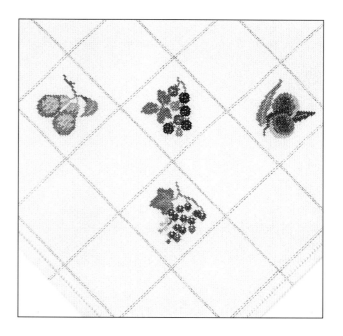

TABLECLOTH

**The finished tablecloth measures
141cm x 94cm (55½in x 37in)**

YOU WILL NEED
*28-count Verona fabric,
152cm x 106cm (60in x 42in)
Stranded embroidery cotton as given in the key
Kreinik metallic blending filaments as given in the key
Matching sewing cotton
No 24 tapestry needle
Sharp HB pencil
Scrap paper
Paper scissors*

This project has been stitched in
DMC six-stranded embroidery cotton and
Kreinik metallic blending filaments

The Embroidery

1 Spread the Verona fabric on a table, so that you can see the arrangement of its metallic squares.

2 Cut 24 small squares of scrap paper and on each write the name of one of the fruits portrayed on my tablecloth. You will need three pieces of paper for each of the eight fruits.

3 Begin in the centre of the tablecloth and, leaving the four central squares blank, arrange one of each of the fruits symmetrically around these squares. I positioned my motifs so that the lower edge of each pattern faced towards the outside edge of the cloth. Tack each piece of paper to the cloth in the appropriate square, using lightly coloured thread.

4 Counting the squares carefully, tack the names of the fruit in the correct positions in each of the four corners of the cloth.

5 Decide which design you are going to begin with. Find the centre of the square, and begin your embroidery at this point.

6 Work the designs over two threads of the fabric, using two strands of embroidery cotton in

the needle. For the parts of the fruit indicated in the key, combine the six-stranded cotton with an appropriate blending filament. Some designs incorporate tall cross stitch. If you need help with this technique see the Leafy Inspiration chapter.

7 When completed, steam press on the wrong side. This is particularly important when working with Kreinik threads, as they should never come

---

Blending Filaments

Metallic blending filaments give a subtle and attractive sparkle to embroidery, and so are ideal for providing the shine on fresh fruits, drenched in morning dew and reflecting the autumn sunshine. Because these blending filaments are very fine and easily damaged, you should use no more than 46cm (18in) of thread at a time. If the thread is too long, it will tend to shred and fray.

As their name suggests, blending filaments are intended to be used in the needle with other threads, such as six-stranded embroidery cotton. They should, however, always be threaded before any other thread, using the following technique to prevent them sliding up and down in the needle.

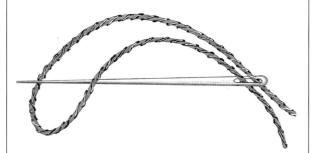

Threading a metallic blending filament

Double the blending filament about 5cm (2in) at one end, and insert the loop through the eye of the needle. Pull the loop over the point of the needle and gently pull the loop towards the end of the eye to secure the thread to the needle. Thread the stranded embroidery cotton through the eye in the usual way, and clip it to match the length of the blending filament.

---

into contact with a hot iron. The heat will damage or discolour them.

Finishing the Tablecloth

This can be done in one of three ways: hemstitch a narrow hem on all sides of the tablecloth (the method I used); machine a hem on all sides of the cloth; or make a fringe all around the cloth.

Method 1: Hemstitching a narrow hem

1 Remove a single thread from the fabric at the hemline.
2 Bring the needle out on the right side, two threads below the drawn-thread line.
3 Working from left to right, pick up two, three or four threads, depending on their thickness (see the Single-Colour Themes chapter). Bring the needle out again and insert it behind the fabric, to emerge two threads down, ready to make the next stitch.
4 Before reinserting the needle, pull the thread tight, so that the bound threads form a neat group.
5 Continue to work around the tablecloth in this way.

Method 2: Machining a hem on all sides of the cloth.

1 Turn in each edge of the tablecloth by 6mm (1/4in), and tack in position.
2 Secure the hem by machine stitching it.

Method 3: Make a fringe all around the cloth.

1 Withdraw a single fabric thread 12mm (1/2in) in from the outer edge.
2 Machine around the rectangle left by the withdrawn threads, using straight stitch or narrow zig-zag stitch.
3 When you have secured the line, remove all cross threads below the stitched line to complete the fringe. Alternatively, you may secure your fringing line by hand, by overcasting every alternate thread.

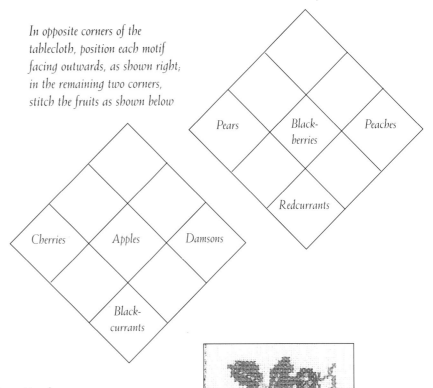

In opposite corners of the tablecloth, position each motif facing outwards, as shown right; in the remaining two corners, stitch the fruits as shown below

Peaches

Redcurrants

Black-berries

Apples

Pears

Damsons

Black-currants

Cherries

Pears

Black-berries

Peaches

Redcurrants

Cherries

Apples

Damsons

Black-currants

Arrange one of each of the fruits symmetrically around the centre of the tablecloth, facing them outwards and leaving the four central squares blank

NOTE Dark lines have been used on the charts to highlight the position of tall cross stitches. These should not be confused with backstitches. There is no backstitching required on any of these designs.

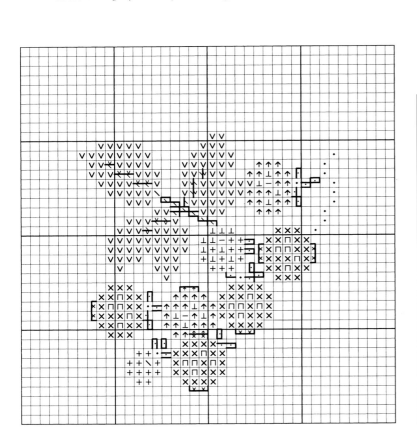

BRAMBLES

		DMC	ANCHOR	MADEIRA
⊟	Ecru	Ecru	926	Ecru
⊓	Navy	823	150	1008
⊠	Black	310*	403*	Black*
↑	Mauve	315	896	0810
⊥	Light mauve	316	895	0809
⊠	Pale green	3348	265	1409
+	Light green	3347	266	1408
∨	Green	3346	257	1407
•	Light brown	840	379	1912

NOTE
* Blend with Kreinik Metallic Blending
Filament black 005

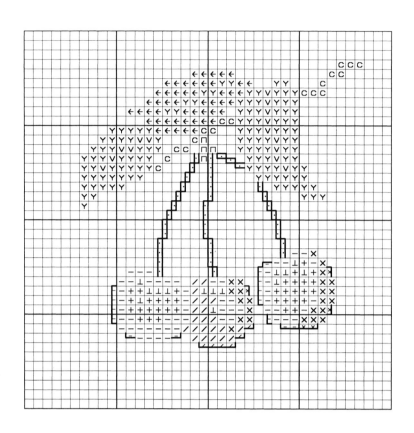

CHERRIES

		DMC	ANCHOR	MADEIRA
☒	Dark red	815	43	0513
⊟	Dull red	304§	47§	0510§
⊞	Red	666§	46§	0210§
⊥	Ecru	Ecru	926	Ecru
←	Dark blue-green	500	879	1705
Y	Blue-green	502	876	1703
V	Light blue-green	504	1042	1701
C	Light brown	840	379	1912
⊓	Dark olive	730	924	1614
·	Yellow-brown	833	874	2203
╱	Maroon	814	44	0514

NOTE
§ Blend with Kreinik Metallic Blending
Filament red 003

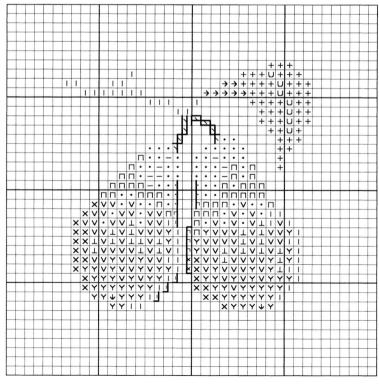

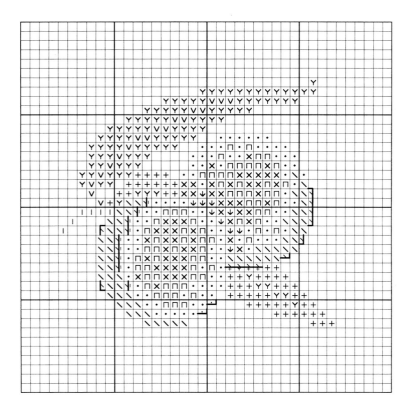

PEARS

		DMC	ANCHOR	MADEIRA
Ⅰ	Brown	610	889	2106
⊟	Cream	3047	886	2205
∨	Gold	725	305	0108
⊠	Red	350§	11§	0213§
⊓	Light red	351§	10§	0214§
⊥	Pink	352	9	0303
⊞	Light green	3347	266	1408
⊌	Pale green	3348	265	1409
→	Dark green	3345	268	1406
·	Yellow-green	734	279	1610
↓	Black	310	403	Black
⅄	Light brown	420	375	2104
⬂	Yellow-brown	833	874	2203

NOTE
§ Blend with Kreinik Metallic Blending
Filament red 003

PEACHES

		DMC	ANCHOR	MADEIRA
⬂	Gold	725	305	0108
⊠	Red	816§	19§	0512§
⊓	Light red	309	42	0507
·	Peach	351	10	0214
⊞	Dark blue-green	500	879	1705
⅄	Blue-green	502	876	1703
∨	Light blue-green	504	1042	1701
Ⅰ	Brown	610	889	2106
↓	Maroon	814	44	0514

NOTE
§ Blend with Kreinik Metallic Blending
Filament red 003

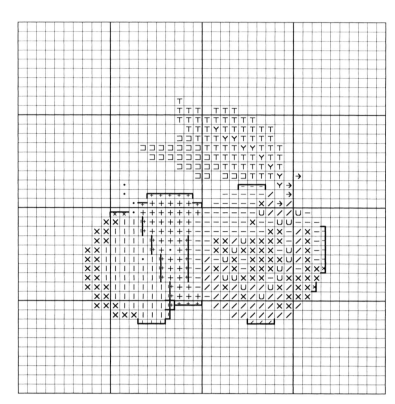

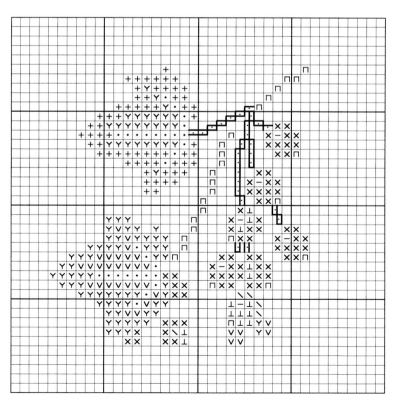

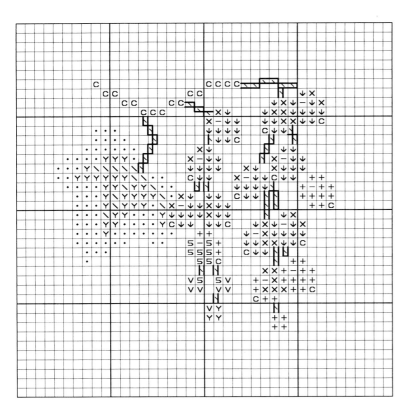

RED CURRANTS

		DMC	ANCHOR	MADEIRA
⊟	Ecru	Ecru	926	Ecru
5	Gold	725	305	0108
☒	Dark red	304§	47§	0510§
↓	Red	666§	46§	0210§
⊞	Light red	350	11	0213
·	Green	3346	257	1407
Y	Light green	3347	266	1408
V	Pale green	3348	265	1409
\	Yellow-green	733	280	1611
C	Light brown	840	379	1912

NOTE
§ Blend with Kreinik Metallic Blending
Filament red 003

DAMSONS

		DMC	ANCHOR	MADEIRA
⊟	Ecru	Ecru	926	Ecru
⊓	Navy	823	150	1008
Ⅰ	Dark blue	791#	941#	0904#
⊠	Blue-purple	333	119	0903
☒	Pink-purple	327	101	0805
\	Yellow-brown	833	874	2203
⊞	Green	3346	257	1407
·	Dark green	3345	268	1406
Y	Pale green	3348	265	1409
V	Light green	3347	266	1408
→	Light brown	840	379	1912
∧	Dark olive	730	924	1614
Z	Black	310	403	Black

NOTE
Blend with Kreinik Metallic Blending
Filament dark blue 033

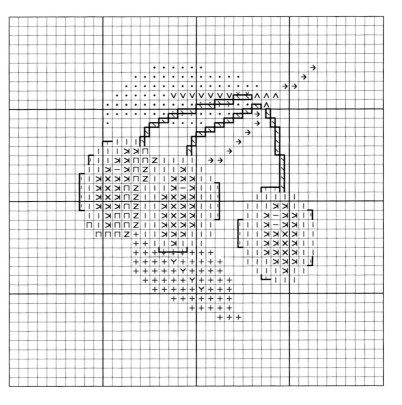

ADAPTING THESE DESIGNS

*B*ecause all these designs will fit into a space 7.5cm x 7.5cm (3in x 3in), they can be used to decorate coasters to match your tablecloth, or the corners of a set of serviettes. If you do not want to embroider a large tablecloth, why not make a set of placemats? These could measure 46cm x 30cm (18in x 12in) and comprise six squares by four squares of the 28-count Verona fabric. The motif would be positioned in the square two from the bottom and two from the left of the placemat. The edges could be hemstitched, machined or fringed.

TRANSFERRING AN IMAGE ON TO FABRIC

In the designs for this tablecloth I have not been able to incorporate all the different fruit found on the Royal Worcester Evesham Gold tableware. In any case, you may wish to design motifs to match the fruit on your own tea or dinner service.

Design Techniques

1 Each block of the Verona fabric contains 78 threads down by 78 threads across, which when working over two threads means space for 39 cross stitches down by 39 cross stitches across. Your piece of graph paper should therefore accommodate a design to fit one of these blocks, but you will also need to allow for a design-free margin of five or six squares all around the fruit.

2 Draw the outline of your fruit, with one or two appropriately shaped leaves, on the plain paper, and try to make the proportions as accurate as possible. Simple fruit shapes are fairly easy to draw and, with a little bit of practice, you will find that your designs begin to look very realistic. Make your drawing bold and keep your lines clear. Remember that your finished embroidery will be only about two-thirds the size of this initial drawing.

The initial pencil sketch of an apple

3 Start to colour the drawing, noticing where the light and dark areas occur and representing them in lighter or darker shades. Where the fruit shape curves away from the light source – around the edge and in the dimple where the stalk joins the fruit – there will be a shadow, and therefore a darker shade of colour is needed. Where the sun or other light source catches the shiny surface of

The original sketch coloured with highlights and shadows

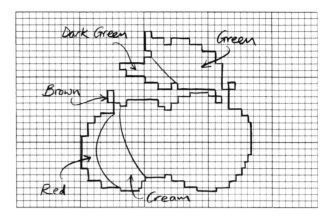

The graph paper drawing with areas for different colours marked

the fruit, there will be a highlight, and you should capture this on paper, too.

4 Place a piece of transparent graph paper over your drawing and secure it with masking tape. Redraw around the outline of your fruit following the shape as closely as possible, but this time moving along the vertical and horizontal lines of the graph paper squares. You may wish to experiment with the tall cross stitch, used horizontally or vertically (see the Leafy Inspiration chapter), to achieve smoother curves for the outline of the fruit.

5 Still following the graph paper grid, mark off the areas of different colours: for example the different reds, yellows and greens on an apple, and the areas of light and shade – not forgetting the highlights.

6 Using your shade card, write in on the appropriate area of your drawing the reference number of your chosen colour. As a rule, it is best to select colours that appear slightly more muted than the original. Too many strong colours, side by side, will not blend together successfully, and and you will not achieve a natural look. A lot of patience, trial and error will be needed to get it right, but as you do more and more designing this process becomes easier.

7 Take the sheet of ordinary graph paper and decide on the positions of each of your designs. Transfer each one using coloured crayons or symbols.

8 Make a key to represent the different colours you will use in your embroidery. When you have done this, it is time to find the centre point of your design and begin stitching.

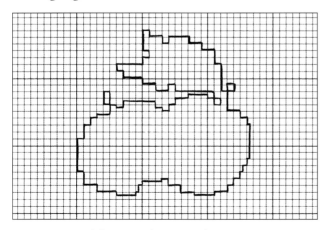

The new outline on graph paper

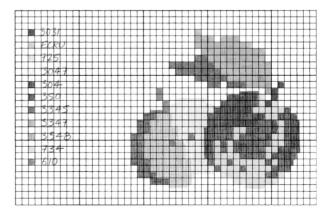

The completed apple chart

SUNFLOWER CHEER

The bold sunflower, immortalised by the well-known, post-Impressionist artist Vincent Van Gogh, brings a touch of warmth into any home. Its botanical name is *Helianthus annuus* and thus it is dedicated to the Greek sun-god Helios. This remarkable plant was cultivated by American Indians around 3,000 years ago, and in the fifteenth century Aztec sun priestesses were crowned with sunflowers, which played an important part in their religious rituals. Sunflowers also featured prominently in motifs used in Aztec gold jewellery. Spanish explorers to the New World discovered the flower and brought it back to Europe in the sixteenth century. Since then it has been cultivated widely, both as an agricultural crop and as an ornamental garden plant. This tall untidy plant, with its big, drooping, golden flower head, peers down on us and brings a smile to our lips.

I was looking for some new bed linen when my eye was caught by a pretty duvet covered with a sunflower design. I thought what a cheering sight it would be to wake up to, and my mind began to explore the possibility of designing some sunflower projects that might complement it. A picture was the obvious choice, but I settled on a more unusual, 'multi-media' picture – employing not just cross stitch but also simple beading and ribbon embroidery as well. A sunflower jewellery box would look good on the dressing table, and I decided it would be a challenge to make the box from fine plastic canvas and decorate it with cross stitch in silky Marlitt thread rather than mount the design in a ready-made box. I then thought a sunflower pendant, in a gilt frame, worked on fine silk gauze, would go well with the jewellery box.

Silk Gauze

Silk gauze is not a material for anyone with poor eyesight, nor for the impatient or faint hearted. However good your eyesight, I would recommend good light and a good magnifying lens for this very fine, silky-textured fabric, and never work for long periods without a break. Your eyesight is precious – so do not abuse it. Available in various counts ranging from 30 to 72, silk gauze is deceptive when you first look at it. The holes, separated by the fine silky grid, appear large and clear. Once you begin to stitch, however, the thread at the back of your work shows through this off-white, almost transparent fabric and makes the location of holes adjacent to where you are stitching very difficult to see.

With silk gauze, each stitch appears like a minute raised bead of colour on a very transparent background. It is therefore essential that no threads should pass across the back of your work, where there are no surface cross stitches to hide them. Unpicking on silk gauze is well-nigh impossible, so you might like to design and stitch your motif on a larger-count material

first. Then when you work it on silk gauze, it will appear like a beautiful little oil painting. Completed motifs can be mounted against any background colour that complements the design.

Mounting Silk Gauze

Since it is such a fine flimsy material, silk gauze must be mounted in a frame before beginning your embroidery.

The simplest method is to mount your small piece of silk gauze centrally in a 7.5cm (3in) plastic clip frame. This will hold the gauze firmly in place, but the main problem is that the depth of the ring allows for little manoeuvrability with the needle when fastening off.

Another method is to buy silk gauze ready mounted in a card frame, or to mount your own in this way. All you need are two small picture mounts, with an aperture a little smaller than your piece of gauze. Lay one mount face down on a firm surface. Place your gauze centrally over it and secure with adhesive tape. Then with strong glue, stick the second mount over the first mount, back to back, with the gauze sandwiched between, and leave under a heavy weight until dry. This is the ideal way to secure your gauze as the mount makes it easy to hold, and there is nothing to hamper the movement of your needle.

If you do not want to go to the trouble of buying picture mounts, and your circular embroidery frame is too large for your piece of silk gauze, you can always machine sew borders of cotton fabric along each edge of your gauze. Insert the whole piece of fabric into the embroidery frame in the usual way.

PENDANT

**The finished pendant measures
3.5cm (1³/₈in) in diameter**

YOU WILL NEED
*40-count silk gauze fabric, 11.5cm x 11.5cm (4¹/₂in x 4¹/₂in)
Stranded embroidery cotton as given in the key
No 26 tapestry needle
Small embroidery hoop, 7.5cm (3in) flexi-hoop or pair of card mounts with apertures less than 11.5cm (4¹/₂in) square
Magnifying glass
A good source of light
Pendant of your own choice*

This project has been stitched in
Anchor six-stranded embroidery cotton

The Embroidery

1 Mount your silk gauze as described opposite.
2 Find the centre of your silk gauze, and the centre of your pattern.
3 Begin your embroidery at this point, using only one strand of embroidery cotton for the cross stitch and backstitch. When working on silk gauze, take care that you do not carry any threads across at the back, except where they are hidden by cross stitches on the surface.
4 When completed, steam press the work on the wrong side if absolutely necessary, but take great care – silk gauze is very fragile.

Finishing the Pendant

1 Mount the work carefully in the pendant. The backing card will show through the silk gauze, so

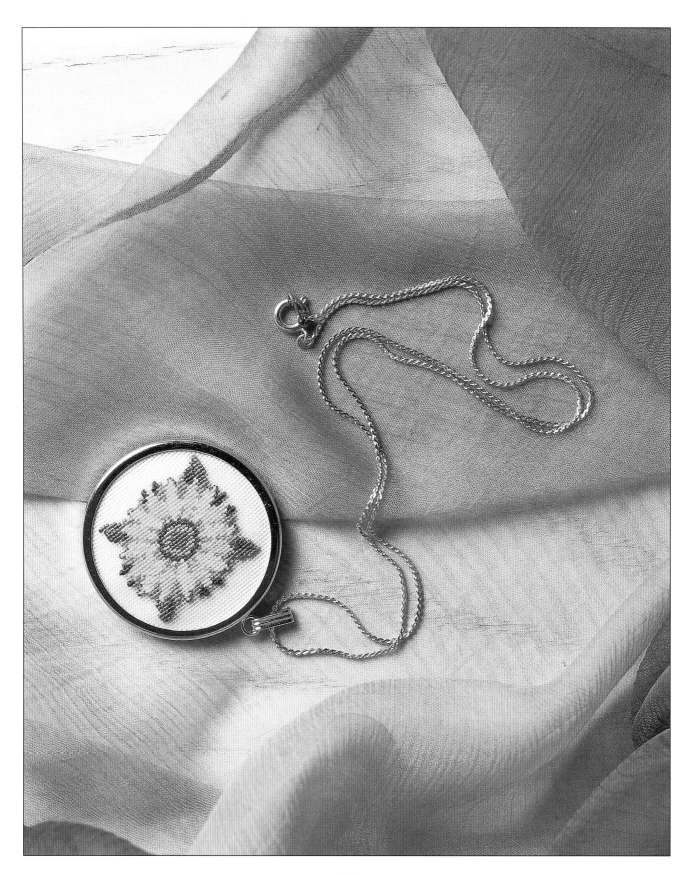

PENDANT

		ANCHOR	DMC	MADEIRA
⊥	Brown	375	420	2104
⊐	Fawn	373	422	2102
→	Dark brown	906	829	2106
⊥	Yellow	298	972	0106
+	Gold	304	971	0203
✕	Light green	267	470	1502
╱	Green	268	937	1504
↖	Dark green	269	936	1507
∨	Lemon	290	973	0105
	Backstitch			
	Brown	375	420	2104

if you want to change its colour, do so now.

2 Bigger pieces can be backed with iron-on interfacing, but the coloured backing card will not then show through the gauze.

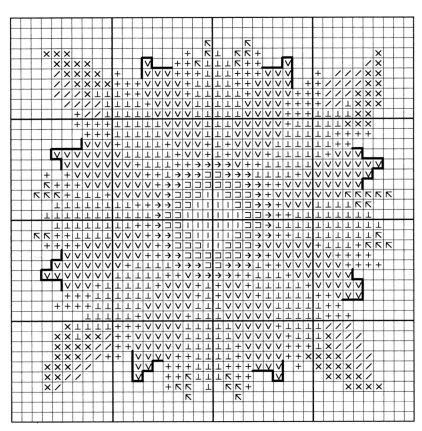

SUNFLOWER BOX

The finished box measures
7.5cm x 7.5cm x 3.5cm (3in x 3in x 1³/₈in)

YOU WILL NEED
1 sheet of 14-count plastic canvas
Soft white lining fabric, 38cm x 38cm (15in x 15in)
Anchor Marlitt and Lamé threads as given in the key
Matching sewing cotton
Strong thread for lacing
No 24 tapestry needle
Sheet of stiff white card, from any good art shop

This project has been stitched in
Anchor Marlitt and Anchor Lamé threads

The Embroidery

1 Cut two pieces of plastic canvas 10cm x 10cm (4in x 4in) for the base and the top of the box, and four pieces 10cm x 6.5cm (4in x 2¹/₂in) for the sides.

2 Begin your embroidery for the top of the box from the centre of the design, using two strands of the Marlitt thread for cross stitch and four strands of the Lamé for both cross stitch and backstitch. The sides and bottom can be embroidered from the edge, but be sure to leave at least one row of holes around the edge of each piece. You will need these to stitch the pieces together.

3 When you have finished the embroidery, trim each piece of the box so that there is a complete row of unused holes around each piece. Cut it very carefully so that the cut edge is smooth.

4 Using three strands of the very dark green Marlitt thread in the needle, stitch each of the four sides

to the bottom of the box, and up each of the four sides, using long-legged cross stitch.

5 Work around the other three edges of the lid and the three top edges of the three remaining sides with blanket stitch, using three strands of very dark green Marlitt in the needle.

Finishing the Sunflower Box

1 Cut six pieces of the card to match exactly the size of the inside measurements of the six component parts of the box. This means that each one will be approximately 3mm (¹/₈in) smaller all the way round than the pieces of embroidered plastic canvas. The lid piece, too, should be slightly smaller than the plastic canvas, so as not to interfere with the hinge, and so as not to come right to the outside edge. There is a lot of trial and error and careful trimming necessary to ensure that they fit exactly.

2 Cut six pieces of lining material large enough to cover the pieces of card and fold over the edges about 12mm (¹/₂in). Lace these to each small piece of the box liner (see Basic Techniques chapter).

3 Stitch the four side pieces to the bottom lining, and lower the complete piece into the box.

4 Glue carefully in place, making sure that no glue comes through on to the right side of the box. Spring-action clothes pegs are useful to hold the lining in position until the glue is dry. In the same way, glue the lining to the lid.

Long-legged Cross Stitch

This stitch, which is also known as long-armed cross stitch, can be used on canvas, plastic canvas and evenweave fabric. It is worked from right to left with the long diagonal stitch running over two spaces whilst the short diagonal stitch is worked over one space, as in ordinary cross stitch. It makes a nice textured edging and can also be used to attach the lid to one side of a box. Here the stitch has an added advantage. Provided it is not worked too tightly, long-legged cross stitch will allow the box lid to open and shut, as on a hinge.

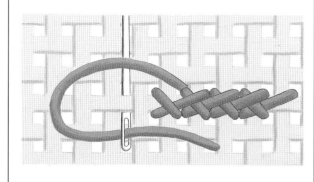

Long-legged cross stitch (a)

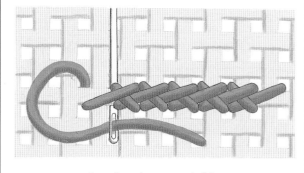

Long-legged cross stitch (b)

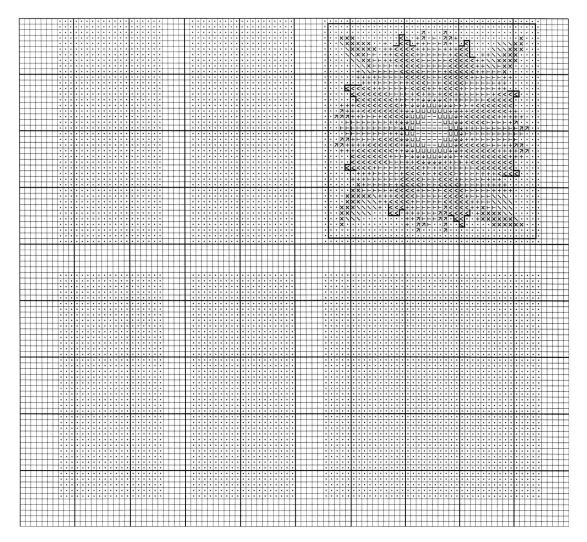

SUNFLOWER BOX

		ANCHOR MARLITT	MADEIRA DECORA			ANCHOR MARLITT	MADEIRA DECORA
⊟	Brown	1140 +Lamé 303	1542 +Lamé 303	◁	Lemon	820	1423
⊔	Fawn	1037	1528		Very dark green (for stitching box together)	853	1570
↓	Chestnut	1040	1456				
·	White*	1212	1471				
⊢	Yellow	821	1525		*Backstitch*		
+	Yellow metallic	Lamé 303	Lamé 303		Yellow metallic	Lamé 303	Lamé 303
✕	Light green	810	1450				
◣	Green	811	1451		*NOTE*		
↗	Dark green	852	1449		* 3 skeins needed		

SUNFLOWER PICTURE

The finished sunflower picture measures
33cm x 10cm (13in x 4in)

YOU WILL NEED
28-count light green Jobelan fabric,
46cm x 23cm (18in x 9in)
Stranded embroidery cotton as given in the key
Matching sewing cotton
Strong thread for lacing
No 24 tapestry needle
Size 10 sharp or beading needle
No 18 Chenille needle for ribbon work
Embroidery frame for use when stitching the ribbon petals
Mill Hill glass seed beads as given in the key
1m (1yd) of 4mm (3/16in) bright yellow silk ribbon
as given in the key
Strong card for lacing the picture
Frame of your own choice

This project has been stitched in
Anchor six-stranded embroidery cotton

The Embroidery

1 Find the centre of your piece of Jobelan fabric, and mark the centre with basting stitches.

2 Find the centre of your sunflower pattern, and from there count up carefully to the centre of your sunflower.

3 From the centre of your Jobelan, count up the appropriate number of threads to the centre of the sunflower – the point to begin your embroidery. (Remember, when counting, that you will be working over two threads of the Jobelan.)

4 Empty a few chestnut-brown beads into a flat dish and sew nine of them in the centre of the flower. Continue with the black beads, and then more chestnut-brown ones, until the middle of the flower is complete. Secure the thread on the back of the work with a couple of backstitches.

Beading

Using a sharp or beading needle and matching thread, secure your sewing cotton at the back of your material, avoiding a bulky knot. Bring the needle through to the right side of your work as though you were going to do a cross stitch. Pick up a bead with the point of your needle and take your needle through to the back of your material, diagonally over two threads, thus completing the half cross stitch.

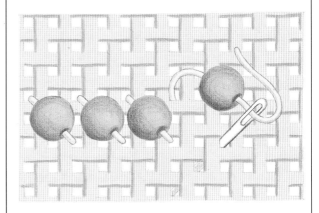

Applying beads

5 Then work all the ribbon petals. To finish, secure the ribbon on the back of your work with a few firm tiny stitches.

6 The bud consists of two French knots and four more small petals. Embroider these and then neatly stitch down the 'tails' of ribbon on the wrong side of your work with a few small stitches.

7 Finish the rest of the sunflower design in cross stitch, using two strands of embroidery cotton, and working over two threads of the fabric.

8 When complete, steam press on the wrong side, avoiding the ribbon and beads.

Finishing the Sunflower Picture

1 Cut a piece of card to fit exactly into your frame.

2 Lace your embroidery on to the strong card (see the Basic Techniques chapter).

3 Insert it into your frame and seal the back.

French Knots

Bring the ribbon out at the required position. Holding the ribbon down with your free thumb, encircle the needle twice with the ribbon. Still holding the ribbon firmly, twist the needle back to the starting point and insert it close to where the ribbon first emerged. Pull the ribbon through to the back of your work and pass on to the position of the next stitch. If you have not tried this technique before, practise on a piece of scrap material.

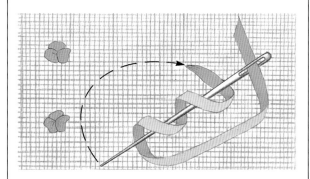

Making a French knot

Ribbon Petals

Even if, like me, you do not usually use an embroidery hoop, you will find one indispensable for ribbon embroidery in order to keep an even tension. One way to secure ribbon in the eye of the tapestry needle is to pass the needle point through the end of the ribbon and pull tightly.

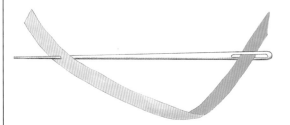

Securing ribbon in a tapestry needle

Insert the needle through the Jobelan fabric at one end of a petal adjoining the flower centre. With the thumb of your free hand, guide your ribbon so that it lies flat along the line of the petal as shown on the pattern, and over the point where you will re-insert the needle. From the right side of your work insert the needle straight down through the ribbon and through the Jobelan. Pull

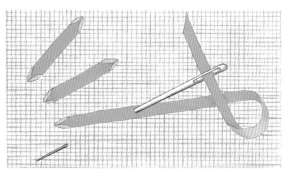

Making ribbon petals

the ribbon very gently down through the hole, until the point where the ribbon was pierced by the needle just passes through the hole. This makes the tip of the petal curl realistically, whilst leaving the rest of the petal lying flat. If you have not tried this technique before, it is best to practise on a piece of waste material before working on a special project.

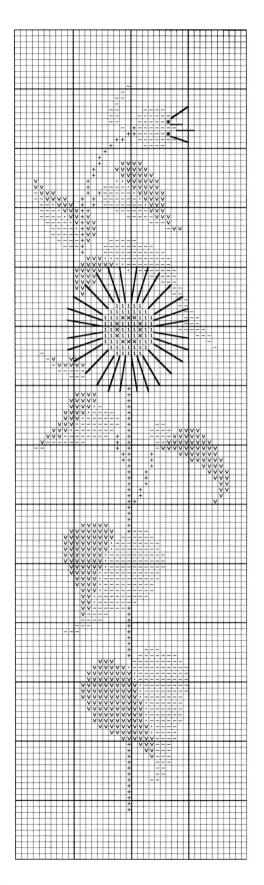

SUNFLOWER PICTURE

		ANCHOR	DMC	MADEIRA
V	Green	268	937	1504
−	Light green	267	470	1502
•	Pale green	265	3348	1409
+	Dark green	269	936	1507

Backstitch
Bright yellow silk ribbon YL1 No 121

Mill Hill glass seed beads

☒	Black		Black
1	Chestnut-brown		00330

DESIGNING FOR CHILDREN

$\mathcal{E}$lephants are loved by children and adults alike. I do not know whether it is their small laughing eyes, their soft sensitive trunks or their big floppy ears, but these gentle giants seem to capture everyone's heart. When I saw a wallpaper border with pastel elephants, I was so enchanted that I was inspired to do some cross stitch designs for children to complement it.

For my first design I chose to do an elephant mobile, consisting of four little elephants in different colours and in varying poses. In these designs I have used features that I thought might appeal to children. The elephants are worked in six-stranded embroidery cotton with fluorescent blending filament, which means that they glow gently in the dark. They also boast 'goggle' eyes, tusks and toe nails created with ivory-coloured or white beads and little bells around their necks as well as tails made from stranded embroidery cotton. Each elephant is suspended on a ribbon from the inside section of an embroidery hoop, bound with ribbon.

The baby's souvenir case continues in the same theme and would make a lovely gift for new parents. This time the elephants with their colourful balloons are embroidered in more traditional fashion on 32-count Belfast linen.

Perforated Paper

The elephants for the mobile are worked on perforated paper, and secured back to back. Mill Hill perforated paper is a very firm, 14-count thin 'card', and is easy to work on. Although the equivalent of 14-count Aida fabric, its proportion of hole to material is much greater. It is gentle on the eyes, and good for those with poor eyesight. It is also excellent for children and those just beginning cross stitch.

For the elephants I chose white perforated paper, but it is available in a variety of colours and metallics. Perforated paper can be cut to any shape, so it makes attractive mounts for photographs or pictures, unusually-shaped cards and bookmarks, and fridge magnets. Its only disadvantages are that you cannot do three-quarter stitch on it and that it is available in only 14 count.

Belfast Linen

The baby's souvenir case is worked on a 100 per cent pure linen, evenweave fabric, which is available in a range of colours, including 'raw' linen. Its fine weave makes it very suitable for delicate designs. Even though Belfast linen is embroidered over two threads, which is similar to working on 16-count fabric, you may need a magnifying glass to work on it comfortably if your eyesight is not good. Being a linen, it has slubs, which means that the fabric threads are uneven in thickness, so special care is needed when counting.

MOBILE

Each of the four elephants measures approximately
10cm x 13cm (4in x 5in) suspended from a
25cm (10in) hoop

YOU WILL NEED
2 sheets of Mill Hill perforated paper
Stranded embroidery cotton as given in the key
Kreinik fluorescent blending filaments as given in the key
Matching sewing cottons
Fine thread for attaching the curtain rings together
No 24 tapestry needle
Sharp HB pencil
8 goggle eyes, 8mm (⅗₆in) diameter
Ivory-coloured or white seed beads
4 small bells
Embroidery hoop, 25cm (10in) diameter
2 curtain rings, 2cm (¾in) diameter
*1m (1yd) each of blue, pink and green ribbon,
1cm (⅜in) wide*
3m (3yd) lemon ribbon, 1cm (⅜in) wide
3m (3yd) white ribbon, 2.5cm (1in) wide

This project has been stitched in
Anchor six-stranded embroidery cotton and
Kreinik fluorescent blending filaments

The Embroidery

1 You may find it easier to begin at the bottom left-hand corner of your chosen elephant design. This will make the most economical use of the perforated paper, and prevent you from running out of space before you have reached the edge of your pattern. Count the holes carefully to the place where you have decided to begin, ensuring that you have at least one complete row of solid squares of perforated paper beyond your embroidery.

2 Thread the needle with two strands of the embroidery cotton together with one strand of the Kreinik fluorescent thread (see the blending filaments box in the Feast of Fruit chapter for how to work with the Kreinik threads). Then

MOBILE

		ANCHOR	DMC	MADEIRA
1	Dull orange	304	741	0201
2	Pale orange	302	743	0113
5	Lemon	288*	445*	0103*
7	Navy	127	939	1009
⊓	Lavender	122	3807	0905
╱	Blue	130§	799§	0910§
↖	Maroon	44	814	0514
⊥	Pink	33#	3706#	0409#
·	Pale pink	778	948	0306
+	Cerise	42	309	0509
→	Dark green	246	986	1404
V	Bright green	243	988	1402
X	Light green	241~	368~	1211~
	Backstitch			
–	Black	403	310	Black

White or ivory-coloured beads

NOTE
* Blend with Kreinik Fluorescent
Blending Filament yellow 054F
§ Blend with Kreinik Fluorescent
Blending Filament white 052F
Blend with Kreinik Fluorescent
Blending Filament pink 055F
~ Blend with Kreinik Fluorescent
Blending Filament green 053F

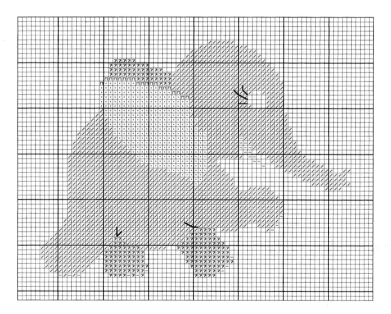

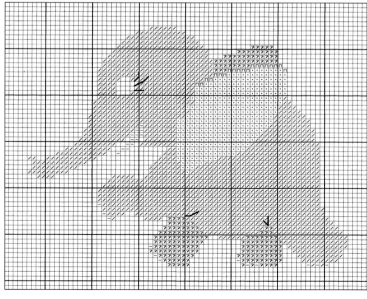

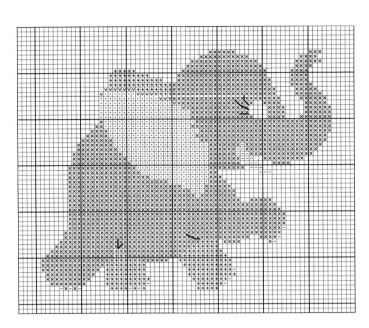

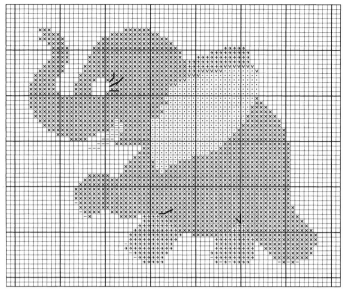

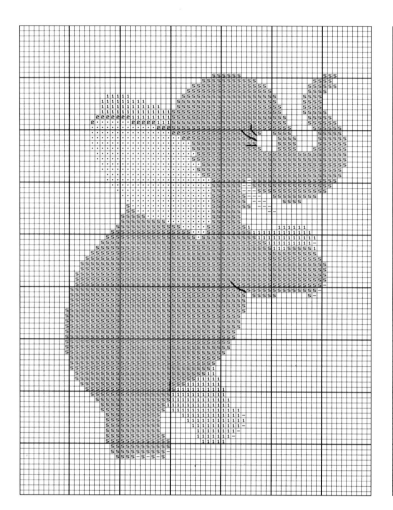

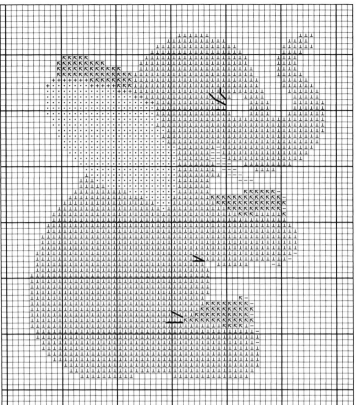

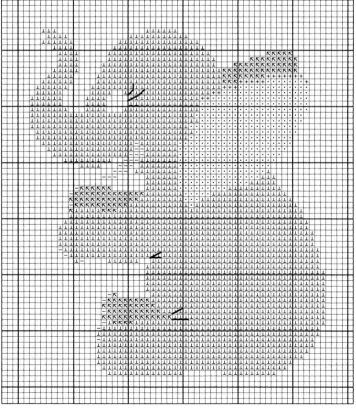

115

start working the body in cross stitch.

3 Add the backstitch using two strands of embroidery cotton.

4 Sew the beads on for the tusks and toe nails, (see the box on beading in the Sunflower Cheer chapter).

5 Mark around the shape of the elephant with the soft pencil, leaving a whole square of perforated paper beyond your stitching, and cut it out carefully.

Finishing the Mobile

1 When you have completed the back and front of an elephant, join the two pieces, back to back, using matching sewing cotton to stitch through the holes around the edge of the elephant. Leave a small gap at the top for the ribbon that suspends each elephant from the hoop.

2 Finish off the elephant by sticking on the eyes, sewing on a bell and a tiny bow under its chin and making a tufted tail from several strands of matching embroidery cotton.

3 Make the other three elephants in the same way.

4 Bind the centre portion of the hoop with white ribbon, and then with the narrower lemon ribbon so that it covers the joins in the white ribbon.

5 Sew the ends of a length of the blue, green, pink and lemon ribbon to one of the curtain rings, from which to suspend the hoop and elephants.

6 Allowing these ribbons to hang down, measure 33cm (13in) along each ribbon and secure each at this point to the hoop, equidistant from one another.

7 From the hoop, measure a further 23cm (9in), and cut off the surplus ribbon.

8 Slip each end of ribbon between the two layers of perforated paper of the appropriately coloured elephant, and stitch into place.

BABY'S SOUVENIR CASE

The finished baby's souvenir case measures 38cm x 23cm (15in x 9in)

YOU WILL NEED
32-count platinum Belfast linen,
70cm x 50cm (27¹/₂in x 19¹/₂in)
Light-coloured lining fabric, 70cm x 50cm (27¹/₂in x 19¹/₂in)
Stranded embroidery cotton as given in the key
Matching sewing cotton
No 26 tapestry needle
Magnifying glass (optional)

This project has been stitched in Anchor six-stranded embroidery cotton

The Embroidery

1 Lay your material out flat and measure up 5cm (2in) from one of the shorter sides. Run a line of basting stitches parallel with this shorter edge and 5cm (2in) from the raw edge of the material. This line marks the bottom row of the border of the design.

2 Find the middle of this line and mark it with a tack. This is the best place to begin your embroidery.

3 Using two strands of embroidery cotton for the cross stitch and backstitch, work the border, then the remainder of the design.

4 When complete, steam press your work on the wrong side.

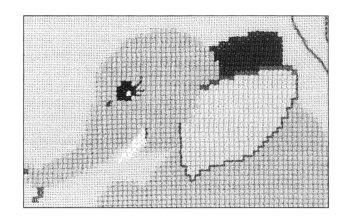

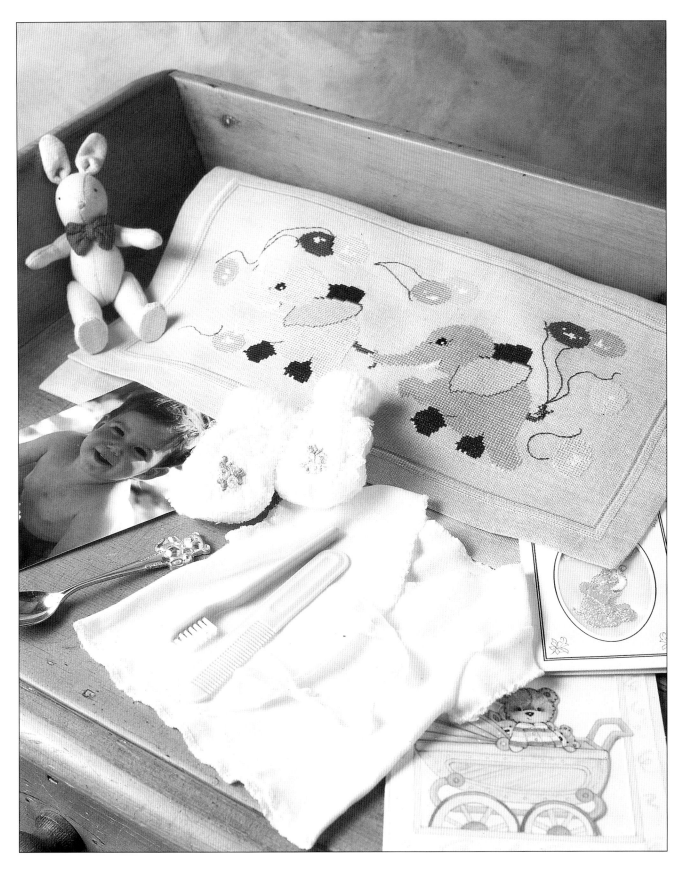

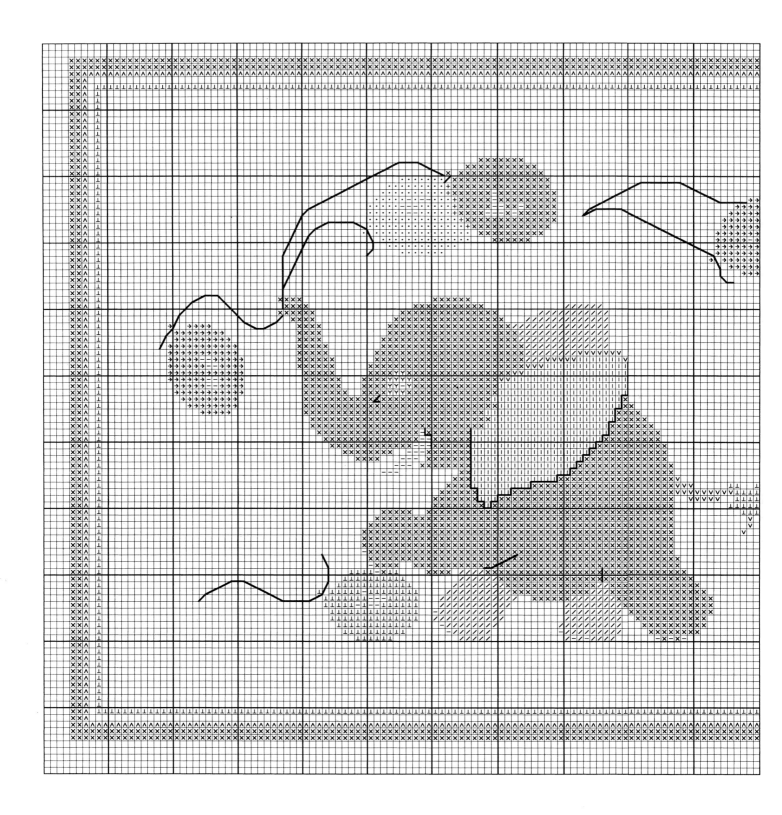

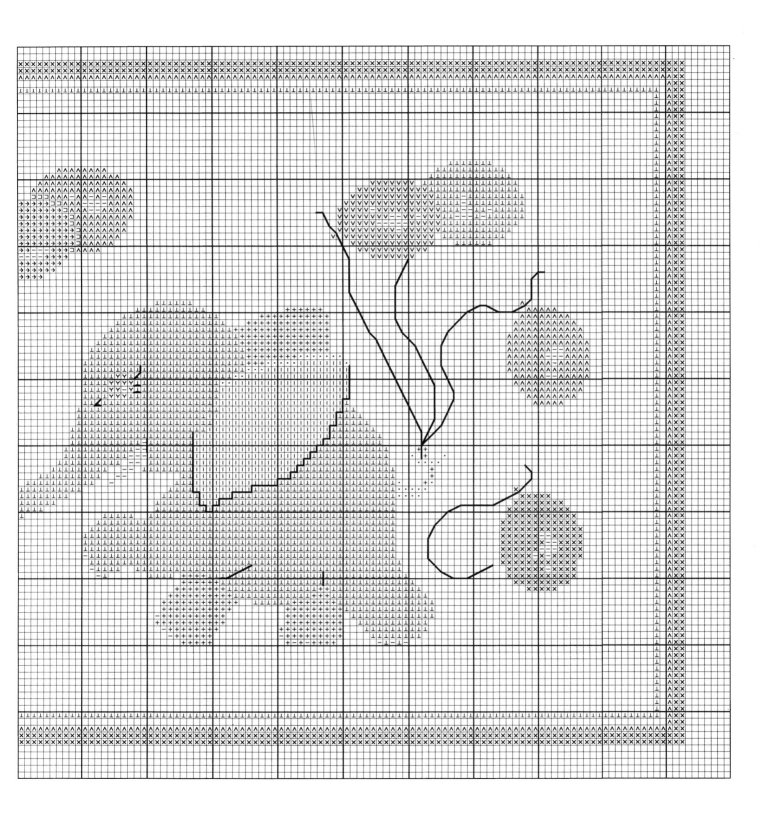

Finishing the Baby's Souvenir Case

1 Trim the embroidered material to measure 66cm x 40.5cm (26in x 16in).

2 Leaving a 19mm (³/₄in) border below, and to the left and right of your design, make a 12mm (¹/₂in) turning all the way around your material. Baste in place. Mitre all four corners.

3 Cut the lining fabric so that it is 66cm x 40.5cm (26in x 16in).

4 Lay the lining fabric over the embroidered linen, wrong sides together, and turn the edges in so that they cover the raw edges of the linen. Slipstitch into place.

5 Hem along the side seams to finish the case.

SOUVENIR CASE

		ANCHOR	DMC	MADEIRA
Y	Black	403	310	Black
⊟	White	1	Blanc	White
⊡	Pale pink	778	948	0306
⋀	Lemon	288	445	0103
⊿	Navy	127	939	1009
⊻	Lavender	122	3807	0905
⊠	Pale blue	128	800	1001
⊞	Maroon	44	814	0514
⊡	Cerise	42	309	0509
⊥	Pink	25	3326	0504
→	Light green	241	368	1211
⊐	Pale orange	302	743	0113
	Backstitch			
	Pink elephant's ear	42	309	0509
	All other backstitch	122	3807	0905

DESIGNING FOR CHILDREN

*R*ather than stitch elephants, you may wish to devise your own motifs based on different childhood favourites. While the small recipient of your embroidery is still very young, you can probably have free rein to choose the characters yourself, whether they be cuddly teddies, farmyard animals, circus clowns or a host of other possibilities. A gift for a child may be just as much a precious keepsake for the mother, so characters and colours chosen with care will complement the other decorative touches in the nursery and give everyone pleasure. Pastels are, of course, ever-popular favourites for babies, but you might consider other alternatives such as fresh sky-blues and sunshine-yellows or bright primaries.

It is not long, of course, before babies become toddlers who are better able to articulate their particular preferences. As they grow older, children are influenced by story books, television and video, and it can often seem hard to keep up with them. Firm favourites can be as wide ranging as fairytale princesses, characterful trains and cars, and even the most gruesome of monsters. You may not like their choice, but you can be sure the child will be delighted with your efforts if you stitch a design featuring their best-loved 'friend'.

Choice of colour is also important here. You may choose to copy faithfully a particular character, or you may decide to use your imagination, choosing subtle blends of soft colours to create a dreamy fanciful world. A bold combination of the two approaches would be an even greater and more stimulating challenge still.

USING TRANSPARENT GRIDS

Whichever characters you eventually select, you should experience little or no difficulty in translating them into a stitched design. If you have drawing skills that is all to the good; if you haven't, you may prefer to trace your characters – but you should do so only if the designs are for your own use, and not for commercial purposes. There are various methods of tracing designs, each with its advantages and disadvantages.

Tracing paper with grids printed on it can be readily obtained from good needlework shops, and you can buy it to match all the most popular counts: for example 10, 11, 14, 16, 18 and 22. These have the advantage of taking the hassle out of making calculations – your design will come out the same size as your drawing on the graph paper. Be aware, however, that when you come to using 18- and 22-count grids, for example, the squares are so tiny that it is impossible to put legible coloured dots or symbols into them. The alternative is to use a bigger squared graph paper, like 10 count, and calculate the size as I have explained in Using Flower Motifs in the Playing with Simple Patterns chapter.

The problem with transparent graph paper is that, however good its quality, the image is never quite clear enough to see the fine detail. The answer to this lies in a relatively new product – acetate grids. These clear sheets of acetate have a grid indelibly printed on them. As with graph paper, various counts are available: 10, 11, 12, 14, 16, 18 and 22. Acetate grids are excellent if you want to trace from photographs – an almost impossible task with transparent graph paper. The difficulty with minute squares on the higher counts is of course the same as with graph paper, but you will find acetate grids invaluable if you are going to design for yourself.

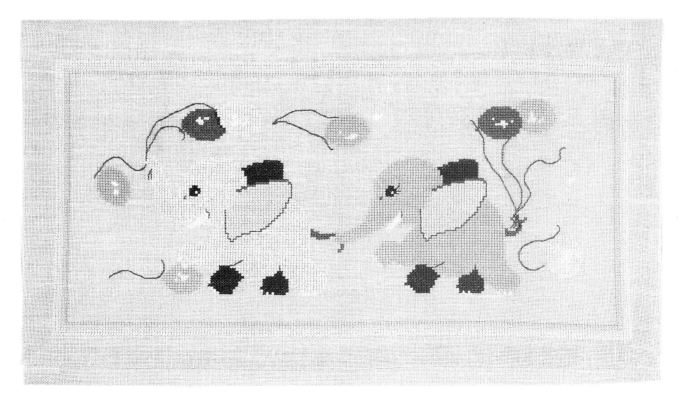

BASIC TECHNIQUES

Preparing the Fabric

Even with an average amount of handling, many evenweave fabrics tend to fray at the edges, so it is a good idea to overcast the raw edges, using ordinary sewing thread, before you begin.

The Instructions

Each project begins with a full list of the materials that you will need. Note that the measurements given for the embroidery fabric include a minimum of 3cm (1¼in) all around to allow for preparing the edges to prevent them from fraying.

Colour keys for the threads are given with each chart. Each of the designs has been stitched with particular threads, and these are given in the first column of each key. Where there is an alternative brand, shades in these thread ranges have also been recommended. The range of shades differs from one brand to another, however, and you may find that where there are two very close shades in the original, it has been necessary to give the same shade for both in another brand. There will always be subtle differences in effect when using a brand other than the original.

It is assumed that you will need to buy one skein of each colour mentioned in a particular key, even though you may use less, but where two or more skeins are needed, this information is included on the colour key.

To work from the charts, particularly those where several symbols are used in close proximity, you may find it helpful to have the chart enlarged so that the squares and symbols

can be seen more easily. Many photocopying services will do this for a minimal charge.

Before you begin to embroider, always mark the centre of the design with two lines of basting stitches, one vertical and one horizontal, running from edge to edge of the fabric.

As you stitch, use the centre lines you have marked on the chart and the basting threads on your fabric as reference points for counting the squares and threads to position your design accurately.

Cross Stitch

To make a cross stitch, bring the needle up from the back of the material at the point at which you wish to begin. Carefully hold the end of the thread as you pull your needle through, and secure the loose end with your first five or six stitches. Never begin with a knot.

For a single cross stitch, as shown below, bring the needle up at hole 1 and down at hole 2 to create the first diagonal stitch. Then bring the needle up at hole 3 and down at hole 4 to complete the cross stitch.

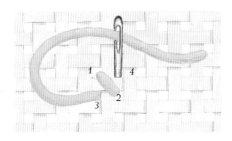

For stitching rows of cross stitch — stitch all the way across, making a row of diagonal stitches, as shown, and then work back, completing each stitch in turn.

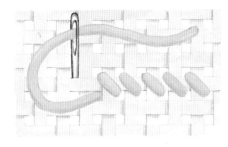

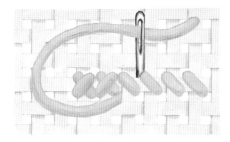

Whether you are making single cross stitches or rows of cross stitches, ensure that all stitches are worked in the same direction.

Backstitch

Backstitch may be used to emphasize a particular line, to give the impression of a slight shadow or to add fine detail to a design. The stitches are either worked as continuous straight lines parallel with the threads of the material, or they are worked diagonally. It is advisable to add the backstitch after all the cross stitching in the same area has been completed.

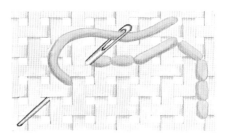

To make a stitch, push the needle up through the material from the back of your work and down through the fabric one stitch length behind the first point. Pass the needle under the material, and then up one stitch length ahead of the first point. Continue in the same way.

French Knots

To work a French knot, bring your needle and thread out slightly to the right of where you want your knot to be. Wind the thread twice around the needle (or three times for a larger French knot) and insert the needle to the left of the point where you brought it out.

Be careful not to pull too hard or the knot will disappear through the fabric.

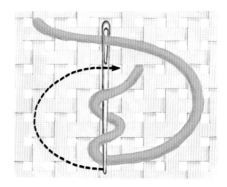

Blanket Stitch

Blanket stitch can be used to create a decorative edge or hem. Hold the fabric in your left hand with the edge towards you and work the blanket stitch from left to right. Hold the thread down with the left thumb. Insert the needle at a hole, without pulling it through. Bring the point of the needle down to the fabric edge, making sure that the loop of thread created goes behind the needle. Pull the needle through so that the cross thread lies against the edge of the fabric.

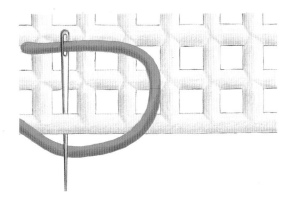

Repeat this process by re-inserting the needle one space to the right of the last stitch. Bring the needle forward through the loop made by the thread from your last stitch. Continue until you have finished your hem.

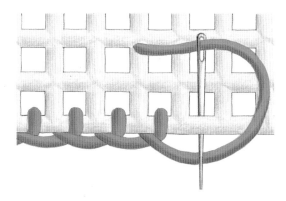

Mitring Corners

Press a single hem to the wrong side of the fabric, the same as the measurement given in the instructions.

Open the hem out again and fold the corner of the fabric inwards as shown in the diagram.

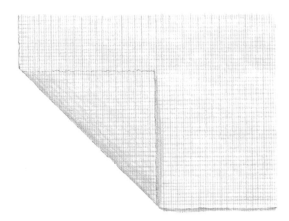

Refold the hem to the wrong side along the pressed line, and trim or fold the corner so that it does not show.

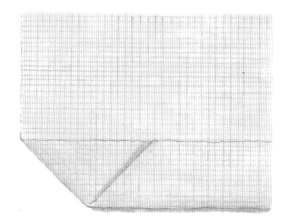

Carefully slipstitch the hem and the mitred corner in place.

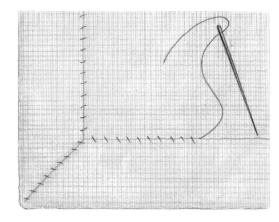

Mounting Embroidery

Cut the cardboard to the size of the finished embroidery, with an extra 6mm (¼in) added all around to allow for the recess in the frame. With a pencil, mark the centre points of each edge of the card.

Lacing Method

A stiff cardboard is needed over which to lace fabrics. This method is recommended for most pieces of work and is essential for heavier fabrics. It produces a sturdy and professional finish.

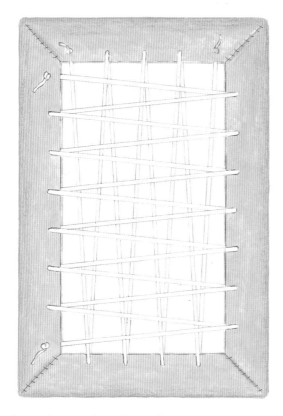

Lay the embroidery face down, with the cardboard centred on top. Match the basting lines on the fabric with the pencil marks on the card. Fold over the edges of the fabric on opposite sides, making mitred folds at the corners, and lace across, using strong thread. Repeat on the other two sides. Finally, pull up the stitches fairly tightly to stretch the fabric firmly over the cardboard. Overstitch the mitred corners.

Quick Method

This method is suitable for lightweight fabrics and where durability is not an important consideration.

Place the embroidery face down, with the cardboard centred on top, and basting and pencil lines matching. Begin by folding over the fabric at each corner and securing it with a small piece of masking tape.

Working first on one side and then the other, fold over the fabric on all sides and secure it firmly with pieces of masking tape, placed about 2.5cm (1in) apart. Also neaten the mitred corners with masking tape, pulling the fabric tightly to give a firm smooth finish.

ACKNOWLEDGEMENTS

I should like to thank my mother, Violet Watts, who made up or assembled all the embroidered articles in this book, and who patiently recorded the steps she took and the processes she employed for inclusion in the instructions for finishing the projects.
I should also like to thank Betty Haste for her help with the checking of charts and proofs at all stages of the preparation of this book.
My thanks are also due to Pauline and Anne of Kaleidoscope needlework and craft materials shop, The Square, Codsall, Staffordshire, who have followed the progress of this book with such interest and have always been at hand with practical help and suggestions.
Thanks, too, to Lyn of Laurel Craft Supplies, Springhill Lane, Wolverhampton, for her encouragement and cheerful support. Her help and advice on all aspects of ribbon work have been so much appreciated.
I am much indebted to MacGregor Designs for the kind gift of the beautifully made footstool and matching box, and to Len and Pat Turner of Fabric Flair, who donated the Jobelan, Salisbury and Verona materials used in this book.
Thanks, too, to Julie Gill of Coats Crafts UK for supplying threads, and regular updates on new products; to Cara Ackerman of DMC, and also to Madeira Threads Ltd, for supplying me with their six-stranded embroidery cottons.
My acknowledgements would not be complete without a sincere thank you to Ian, Martin and Kirsty of IL-SOFT, Specialist Craft Software, Witney, Oxfordshire, for help and advice concerning the use of their excellent cross stitch design programs.
Finally, I must express my appreciation to my long-suffering friends and neighbours who follow the creation of my designs with such interest, and who must wonder where I disappear to for months at a time. Especially, I should like to thank Peter Jones, who created my new office and workroom in which this book was born.

The publishers would like to thank Coats Crafts UK, DMC, Fabric Flair and Madeira Threads for supplying materials for photography in this book.

SUPPLIERS

For information on nearest stockists of embroidery threads in the UK

Coats Crafts UK,
(for Anchor threads)
McMullen Road, Darlington,
Co Durham DL1 1YQ
Tel. 01325 381010
(also distributors of Kreinik blending filaments)

DMC Creative World Ltd,
Pullman Road, Wigston,
Leicestershire LE18 2DY
Tel. 01162 811040
(also distributors of Zweigart fabrics)

Madeira Threads UK Ltd,
Thirsk Industrial Park,
York Road,
Thirsk,
North Yorkshire YO7 3BX
Tel. 01845 524880

For information on nearest stockists of embroidery threads in the USA

Coats & Clark Inc,
PO Box 24998,
Greenville,
SC 29616–2498

The DMC Corporation,
Port Kearney Building,
10 South Kearney,
NJ 07032–0650

Madeira USA Ltd,
30 Bayside Court,
PO Box 6068,
Laconia,
NH 03246

For information on nearest stockists of embroidery threads in Australia

Coats Patons Crafts,
Thistle Street,
Launceston,
Tasmania 7250

DMC Needlecraft Pty Ltd,
PO Box 317,
Earlswood,
NSW 2206

Penguin Threads Pty Ltd,
25–27 Izett Street,
Prahran,
Victoria 3181

For information on nearest stockists of embroidery fabrics (Jobelan, Verona, Salisbury and Aida)

Fabric Flair,
Unit 3,
Northlands Industrial Estate,
Copheap Lane, Warminster,
Wiltshire BA12 0BG
Tel. 0800 716851

For transparent acetate grids

Creative Grids,
PO Box 207,
Leicester LE3 6YP
Tel./Fax 01162 857151

For pendants, key fobs and wooden rods for samplers

Framecraft Miniatures Ltd,
372–376 Summer Lane,
Hockley,
Birmingham B19 3QA
Tel. 0121 212 0551

For footstools and matching boxes

MacGregor Designs,
PO Box 129,
Burton upon Trent DE14 3XH
Tel./Fax 01283 702117

For bells and bellpull fittings

Crafts By Design Ltd,
Needlepoint House,
28 Ederoyd Drive, Pudsey,
West Yorkshire LS28 7RB
Tel. 01532 574102

For keyboxes

S & A Frames,
The Old Post Office,
Yarra Road, Cleethorpes,
North Lincolnshire DN35 8LS
Tel. 01472 697772
Fax 01472 697557

For Framecraft stockists worldwide

Anne Brinkley Designs Inc,
12 Chestnut Hill Lane, Lincroft,
NJ 07738, USA

Danish Art Needlework,
1217 Center Street N, Calgary,
Alberta T2E 2R3, Canada

Ireland Needlecraft Pty Ltd,
2–4 Keppel Drive, Hallam,
Victoria 3803, Australia

The Embroidery Shop,
286 Queen Street, Masterton,
New Zealand

Sanyei Imports,
2–64 Hirakata Fukuju–Cho,
Hashima Shi Gifu, Japan

INDEX